"I'm grateful for Chad Lunsford heart. He's written a timely book that will inspire you to dig a little deeper, take a few more calculated risks, and do the necessary work to embrace the unique purpose God has in mind for you. In a world desperately looking for hope, you'll find plenty of it on the pages of this book."

—AARON BROCKETT,
Lead Pastor of Traders Point Christian Church

"Chad Lunsford's *Made for More* is a powerful reminder that we were not meant to play it safe in life. This book inspires us to discover our purpose and live with intention. I highly recommend this inspiring book!"

—STEVE SACCONE,
Author and Vice President of Ministry Network at Southeastern University

"In his book, *Made for More*, Chad helps us unlock and realize our God-given potential. His words aren't based on theory or hypothetical thought. They are forged through the wisdom of his experience. This book is your guide to walking in deeper faith, and discovering your most extraordinary story is still being written."

—JUSTIN DAVIS,
USA Today Bestselling Author of *Being Real > Being Perfect*,
Founder of RefineUs Ministries

"I, like a lot of people, tend to jump just high enough to clear whatever bar is in front of me. In *Made For More*, Chad has encouraged me to look for a higher bar, to believe in more than whatever low bar the world has set. If you're looking for a fresh perspective that will expand your thinking, pick up a copy today."

—WILLIAM VANDERBLOEMEN,
CEO and Founder of Vanderbloemen, Author of *Be The Unicorn*

"In a world that often encourages us to settle for mediocrity, *Made for More* by Chad Lunsford is a breath of fresh air. This book challenges us to step out of our comfort zones and pursue our true calling."

—JASON JAGGARD,
Founding Partner of Novus Global,
and *USA Today* Bestselling author of *Beyond High Performance*

"If you've ever felt like there's more to life than what you're currently experiencing, *Made for More* by Chad Lunsford is the book for you. It's a compelling journey that will reignite your passion and encourage you to live your life to the fullest. Chad has exhibited this kind of living in his own life, and his journey validates the very path he challenges us to live."

—TIM SMITH,
Senior Executive Pastor of Lakepointe Church

"All the noise around our lives has a way of deafening us to the purpose God has for our lives. Chad Lunsford's message in *Made For More* is like a megaphone that will capture your attention, practically pointing you to a life of more meaning, purpose, and significance."

—STU HODGES,
Founder and Lead Pastor, Waters Edge Church

"In *Made for More*, Chad Lunsford delivers a powerful message of hope and inspiration. This book is a roadmap for those who want to break free from the status quo and live a life that reflects their true purpose and the character of God."

—TIM STEVENS,
Founder of LeadingSmart and Author of *Marked By Love*

"Chad is an incredible communicator who desperately wants people to uncover who God made them to be. He has a fresh, optimistic mindset that awakens people of all types. These audacious words will get you unstuck!"

—ALAN BRIGGS,
Author and Leadership Coach, Founder of Stay Forth coaching network

"*Made for More* is a concise road map to help you live into the fullness of your calling and guide you past the roadblocks that can slow you down. Chad Lunsford makes a compelling case that we can reach our God desired destinations by making some strategic adjustments in how we follow Jesus. I recommend this book for anyone who has ever felt stuck in neutral on their journey through life."

—ERIC RAUCH,
Executive Pastor at 2|42 Community Church

"For all of us there are seasons of distressing doubt when we long to believe there's more. Those seasons are fraught with too many questions and too few answers. Chad has lived those seasons. He's done the work and asked the difficult and right questions. This is his story of discovering and living into the reality of being made for more. And his story is an insightful guide to helping each of us navigate our own story to discover our core identity, that we were made for more."

—MARK WALTZ,
Leadership Coach and Organizational Consultant

REACH YOUR HIGHEST PURPOSE
& LIVE YOUR GREATEST STORY

MADE for MORE

CHAD LUNSFORD

FOREWORD BY MARK BATTERSON
NEW YORK TIMES BESTSELLER

Fedd Books
P.O. Box 341973
Austin, TX 78734

www.thefeddagency.com

Published in association with The Fedd Agency, Inc., a literary agency.

ISBN: 978-1-957616-90-2
eISBN: 978-1-957616-60-5

LCCN: 2024901922

Printed in the United States of America

This book is dedicated to my wife, Katie, and our kids, Ava, Ella, and Aidan. You fill the pages of my story with beauty, joy, laughter, and adventure. May this book guide your great stories.

CONTENTS

FOREWORD

God has a way of teaching us life's most important lessons at the most inopportune times. Or so it seems, at the time. But it's when we feel unsettled, when the tectonic plates of life are shifting, that God is doing His deepest work.

When I was nineteen years old, I asked God a dangerous question: *what do you want me to do with my life*? The only thing more dangerous than asking that question is *not* asking that question! After many months of seeking God, I felt called to full-time ministry. At the time, I was a pre-law major with a full-ride scholarship to the University of Chicago. I made a very difficult decision to give up that scholarship and transfer to a Bible college to pursue ministry. It made no sense on paper, but it's one of the best decisions of my life.

It was during that season of transition that I learned some valuable lessons. One, the greatest risk is taking no risks! If you want to walk on water, you have to get out of the boat. Two, quit living as if the purpose of life is to arrive safely at death. Live your life in a way that is worth telling stories about. Go after a dream that is destined to fail without divine intervention.

In February of 2021, I was talking with my friend, Chad Lunsford. He was facing an incredibly difficult decision, and his life was in transition. He felt called to write a book, but writing a book felt like Mount Everest. I asked Chad if he was called to write. He answered in the affirmative. So I said to Chad, "Then not writing is disobedience." Faith is taking the first step before God reveals the second step, and I challenged Chad to take that first step. To Chad's credit, that's exactly what he did. Over the subsequent nine months, Chad offered updates on the writing process. The book you hold in your hands is the last step in the writing journey, but make no mistake, it started with the first step!

The same is true for you.

You were made for you!

As Chad writes in the coming pages, the journey to destiny is never a straight line! Soon after Chad completed this manuscript, he and his wife, Katie, sensed God leading them to transfer leadership of the church they planted. They took their first sabbatical as a family, and they began *Made For More,* a non-profit ministry designed to help individuals and organizations reach their God-given potential.

Potential is God's gift to you. What you do with it is your gift back to God.

As only God can orchestrate, exactly two years after we prayed together on that first video call, Chad signed on with Fedd Books to publish this book. The world needs this book, needs this message. There is a longing in all of us for more, but that longing must be well-managed. It can't be more *things.* You were made for more—more love, more passion, more purpose, more meaning. And the path to more involves overcoming inevitable obstacles. The good news? The obstacle is not the enemy. The obstacle is the way. You cannot spell testimony without the first four letters. You have to pass the test in order to get the testimony! This book will help you do just that.

I have no idea where you are in life's journey, but I am confident that there is a next level. Why? Because there is no finish line! You have untapped potential. You were made to live, made to act, made to serve, made to reflect, made to soar.

It's time for takeoff.

Mark Batterson
NYT Bestseller

"The place God calls you to is the place where your deep gladness and the world's deep hunger meet."

——FREDERICK BUECHNER[1]

DON'T SETTLE

I didn't make the cut.

I remember reading the results like it was yesterday.

My third-grade teacher had recommended that I be tested for a new gifted and talented program created by our local school system. If my scores were high enough, I'd be accepted, which also meant I'd have to move schools. I didn't like the thought of leaving my friends, but I loved the idea of being extraordinary.

My scores were high, but not high enough. What I heard was, "You're not good enough." I wanted to be outstanding, but you can't argue with scores. Mundanity was my destiny. I thought my chance at being exceptional had passed me by.

From that point forward, school was no longer important to me. Two decades later, I'd enroll as a post-graduate student at Duke University. But I promise you this: Not one of my high school teachers or undergraduate professors would have seen that coming.

When I couldn't stand out in education, I tried athletics. But there was always someone more skilled, taller, faster, and stronger. And while I loved my childhood, my commonplace surroundings seemed to affirm my common accomplishments. I was born in a small midwestern town, and my house sat in the middle of commercial farmlands. The "big city" nearby was renowned for being *the* Crossroads of America, with a plaque and all. We're famous for being in the middle. Jetsetters bouncing from one big city to another would label us a "fly-over state."

I've often felt at war with myself. While there's a voice beckoning me to live an extraordinary life, there are other voices persuading me to expect less, play it safe, and dream smaller. I guess it's in my DNA. My forefathers began as pioneers, but eventually they became settlers.

I suspect that you feel the same tug of war within yourself. While the internal and external influences clamor for a hearing, there's another voice summoning you to a life of purpose, a great story, a life worth living. Part of you thinks that you should settle. And yet, there's a purpose within you, waiting to emerge. I understand the pull, and I want to beg you from the start of this book: please, don't settle! We need you to live fully. You have too much greatness within you to settle for less.

MY BIBLE FELL APART

Discovering the source of the beckoning voice was more than a bit surprising. Some of my earliest childhood memories are lying awake late at night, wondering if God exists, unsure of how to find out. Are heaven and hell real places? Do I have a reason for being here? Can someone answer my questions or help with my inner hurt? I was desperate to learn about this man named Jesus, but I was wary of Christians. I didn't understand what I saw on TV, I feared what I read on billboards, and the few Christians I knew seemed so serious or strange.

Also, to my surprise, a close friend attended church services weekly and invited me to join them. Despite my concerns, I jumped at the opportunity.

I was afraid that my clothes would be judged, I'd say the wrong things, or I'd sit in someone's seat. Gratefully, I found a beautifully imperfect group of people who loved me where they found me. Rather than demanding outward behavior changes, they just displayed how their internal faith grew into outward expressions of love. I was afraid I wouldn't belong, but everything they did said, "Welcome home!" And I loved how the pastor shared the Bible's relevance to our daily lives. The more I encountered the scriptures—beyond simply getting answers for my questions – my soul was finding its Maker. I was afraid that Jesus and the Bible were outdated and driven by rules. I discovered that the Bible is actually life giving, and that Jesus Himself was the voice inviting me to live fully.

Then, one day, my Bible fell apart. And I mean that literally. From Philippians 3 to Revelation 22, the pages fell apart and scattered. As a college student, I was so captivated by that Philippians chapter, and one verse specifically, that I persistently returned to it. The constant opening, highlighting, and underlining eventually took its toll.

Paul was writing a letter to followers of Jesus in the city of Philippi. In it, he detailed how his lofty life goals before meeting Jesus were self-centered and short-sighted. Now, he desired to fully live into his calling. Then, he wrote the verse that resonates so deeply with my soul: "Not that I have already attained, or am already perfected; but I press on, that I may lay hold of that for which Christ Jesus has also laid hold of me" (Philippians 3:12 NKJV). Almost daily I would return to this chapter. Paul found his selfish pursuits left him empty but discovered divine purpose in following Jesus. Paul understood that Jesus died so that he could live. He desired to "lay hold of that for which Christ Jesus also laid hold of" him.

Like Paul, I've discovered immense joy in living out a life of purpose. As a college student, I didn't know much about Paul, Jesus, or the Bible, but I understood the search for significance. Because you're reading this book, I'm guessing that you're searching for it, too.

DISCOVER YOUR HIGHEST PURPOSE

As loud as the internal and external voices can be, I want to awaken you to another voice that continually summons you forward. Beyond the mundane, there is a life of passionate purpose, a life of impact on the people around you, a life truly worth living. Paul teaches that God intentionally created you and me to bring about a purpose on this earth. And while brokenness in the world holds us back, the life and death of Jesus retrieves and redeems it for every person that places their faith in Him.

Over and over, I read those words.

"Not that I have already attained," Paul said, "but I press on, that I may lay hold of that for which Christ Jesus laid hold of me."

Jesus grabbed hold of me, and now my life can grab hold of that reason He died to give me life. Since those early days of being transfixed on these words, I have desired a life of purpose. I've dared to discover my highest purpose. Regardless of where you are on your journey, you can too. It's never too late to start. You aren't behind and you haven't derailed God's plan. Right now, right where you are, you can begin discovering God's purpose for your life. In the five sections of this book, I've identified five attributes that comprise your divine design. When you put these attributes into practice, you'll discover your highest purpose.

LIVE YOUR GREATEST STORY

There are some things that you simply *must* do. Writing this book is a *must* for me. I'm not writing it because I've arrived, or because I'm an expert on the subject of living fully. I'm writing it because I *must*. This book is scream-ing from within me to be heard. It's my story, but I have a suspicion that it's your story, too.

I've designed this book to help you take meaningful steps toward laying hold of your greatest story. I want to embolden and empower you to run after life truly worth living. I'll share personal stories and discoveries from my own pursuit of purpose. This is a book that you can return to at different stages in your life journey. In fact, don't see the sections of this book as a ladder to climb but a cycle to continually grow and live out.

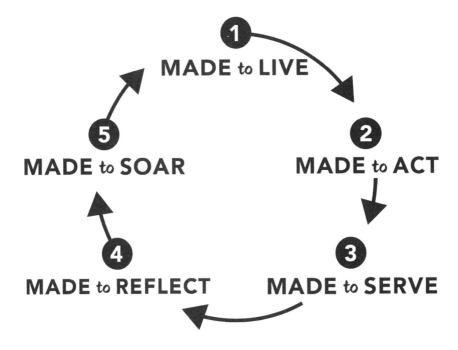

The five sections of the book unfold the five attributes that comprise a made-for-more life. They can help you identify where you are and the next steps to be taken. As you become familiar with the attributes, you can recognize what's missing or where growth is needed and use the book as a guide toward discovering new facets of your God-given purpose. As you embody the five attributes, you'll learn to overcome common obstacles so that you can live your greatest story.

In Attribute One, you'll wake up to who God created you to be, beating fear and destroying lies that hold you back. As you discover that you're made to live, you'll learn how to seize divine moments and reclaim truths about your life while passionately pursuing risks worth taking.

Then, in Attribute Two, you'll move with purpose to reverse weariness, crush inaction, and eradicate escapism. Encountering vision-centered perseverance, faith-filled action, and purposeful wandering, you'll begin to live with a made-to-act mindset.

Next, in Attribute Three, you'll take meaningful steps toward making a real difference with your life as you defeat distraction, smash selfishness, and axe apathy. As you recognize that you are made to serve, you'll begin to take ground with relentless focus, self-giving courage, and divine confidence.

In Attribute Four, you'll discover how you are made to reflect your Maker. Your life will grow at the pace of your character, so you'll learn to fortify your soul by expanding your character. Therein, this attribute will guide you to grapple greed, prune pride, and extinguish entitlement as you cultivate gratitude, generosity, integrity, and wholeness.

Finally, Attribute Five will empower you to take big strides into the life you were created to live. As you discover that you are made to soar, you'll feel freedom to run your race and make daily progress.

MADE FOR MORE

Throughout this book, people in the Bible will become our travel companions not because they always get it right but because they offer their lives back to God when they get it wrong. You will discover why the lives of imperfect people like David and Peter resound so deeply in your own soul. If you assume that people in the Bible always get it right, you miss the point entirely. They were flawed just like us. Yet God used them, and God desires to redemptively work in your life too.

I'm guessing that you have some questions about faith. You have doubts and frustrations. Perhaps you don't feel like you belong in faith communities. I'm a pastor and even I can resonate with each of these. But don't let these stop you from venturing forward. Let these questions fuel your resolve. You don't have to be a Christian to read this book, you don't have to believe what I believe, and you don't have to attend a church. My faith today is the result of decades of searching, exploring, risking, and growing.

Paul's pursuit has become my own—to lay hold of that for which Christ Jesus laid hold of me. I believe with my whole being that Jesus surrendered His life so that I could be forgiven. Jesus burst forth from the grave so that I could be made new. Jesus has laid hold of me. Now, my response is to lay hold of the life that He purposed for me. I choose to run after it. To overcome all obstacles to reach it. What about you?

When Jesus conquered death, He made it possible for all of us to be redeemed of our broken pasts, to overcome the challenges in our lives, and to be empowered to pursue our unique God-given purpose. In fact, God wants you to pursue it. God desires that you discover His purpose for your life. Jesus died so that you can be freed from what holds you back. Jesus rose from the dead so that you can live fully. You *can* lay hold of it.

You are made for more.

ATTRIBUTE 1
MADE *to* LIVE

Defeat Fear, Destroy Lies, Discharge Failure

". . . Awake, O sleeper, rise up from the dead . . ."
—Ephesians 5:14

"The credit belongs to the man . . . who spends himself in a worthy cause; who at the best knows in the end the triumph of high achievement, and who at the worst, if he fails, at least fails while daring greatly, so that his place shall never be with those cold and timid souls who neither know victory nor defeat."

—THEODORE ROOSEVELT[2]

CHAPTER 1

REACH OUT AND CATCH LIFE

It was just a few months after we dropped anchor in Pasadena, California, at the base of the Sierra Madre mountains, and I was walking up the steps to our apartment complex. We lived just a couple of blocks north of Colorado Boulevard (a great place to live if you want to appreciate the annual Rose Bowl Parade). As I reached the top step, I could see something bouncing toward me from the courtyard. It kept bouncing right through the gate toward me. Just before it passed me by, I reached out my left hand and caught it. I caught a bouncing ball. You know, one of those multi-colored, only-cost-a-quarter at the grocery store, twist-the-vending-machine, "Child's Best Day Ever" bouncing balls. Then I heard Katie's voice: "Ava, Daddy caught your ball!"

"Daddy caught my ball," Ava exclaimed. "Daddy caught my ball!"

Until I heard them, I hadn't noticed my wife and daughter in the courtyard. *What are the chances*, I thought to myself, *that at the exact moment my daughter would wildly throw a bouncing ball, I would emerge from Madison Avenue and catch it?* This was special. As they ran over, I triumphantly proclaimed with them, "Daddy caught your ball!"

I handed the treasure to Ava, certain that she'd desire a banquet to be thrown in my honor. Instead, she swiftly launched it down the steps. I ran down and once again saved the ball from its ill-fated demise in a Pasadena storm drain. Ava again applauded my heroics. I wasn't as excited. I bent over, looked her in the eye, and declared, "Sweetie, I don't want you to lose this. Why don't you put it in your pocket to keep it safe?" I didn't fully understand it at the time, but her innocent joy had turned to fear.

MADE TO BOUNCE

Sometime later, I emerged from studying in my "office," which was really a tiny corner of our bedroom outfitted by Ikea. I asked Ava if she wanted to play with her bouncing ball in the courtyard, but I wasn't prepared for her answer.

"No, Daddy," she angrily replied. "You told me to put it in my pocket to keep it safe!" Though I kept pushing, she dug in her heels. War with a toddler, especially against my independent Ava, is not for the faint of heart. Thus, I decided not to dig my trench and mount a counteroffensive.

During dinner, Katie smiled at me and said, "You're not going to believe this, but she will not get that ball out of her pocket." When I told Ava to put the ball in her pocket, I simply didn't want to chase it again down Madison Avenue. Before then, it had never occurred to her that she could lose it. I had placed fear in her mind, and now I was determined to restore wonder in her heart.

After dinner, Ava and I returned to the courtyard where most nights were spent playing and laughing. Living on the ground floor in our tiny apartment, this concrete jungle was an extension of our urban home. On this night, I bent down on one knee and looked into Ava's dark brown eyes. Once more I asked if we could throw the bouncing ball, and once more, she scolded me:

"No, Daddy! You said I should keep it safe!"

Then it occurred to me, not once but twice, I had rescued this ball for her. Now, she was withholding from me the very thing I had saved for her, which is exactly what we do with God. How many times do we bounce wildly out of control, only to be rescued by our good Father? And yet, when fear grows in our hearts, we withhold our lives from the very One who desires to rescue us.

"I know, sweetie," I replied. "I'm really sorry. I didn't mean to scare you."

This caught her attention. I had touched on the emotion that she was most feeling.

"Avabean," I continued. "This ball was made to bounce. It wasn't meant to be kept in your pocket. You should bounce it and have as much fun with it as you can." She was listening. "If you'll let me see it," I suggested, "I'd like to show you how high it can go."

I could sense that Ava was afraid to throw it herself, but perhaps she trusted me enough to bounce it. In fear and trepidation, she reluctantly reached into her tiny pocket, grabbed the bouncing ball, and lifted it up to me.

A smarter dad may have taken his time, but I decided to act fast. I stood, raised the ball high over my head, preparing to slam it against the concrete. I caught Ava's eyes, and they were silently screaming, "Noooo, Dad!" But it was too late. I smashed the bouncing ball against the ground, and it rocketed into the sky. That's when I noticed how dark it had become outside, because when I looked up, I couldn't see the ball. That's right. I had finally coaxed the bouncing ball from Ava's pocket, launched it into the night sky . . . and I was on the brink of losing it forever—along with her confidence in me.

Now, in my defense, the night sky in Los Angeles is pitch black. To complicate things more, the immense light pollution drowns out the stars and any chance for nuance as you look up. However, this was no time for establishing my defense—I had to find the ball. I desperately scanned the sky and in the last second, saw the ball, reached out, and caught it. And as if I planned it this way, I caught it right in front of Ava's face. Her eyes widened as she looked up at me. "Daddy, do it again!" Wonder had been restored!

Over the next several minutes, I would again slam the ball against the concrete, it would get lost in the night sky, only to reemerge, and we'd chase it all over the courtyard. As magical as this was, this was not the redemption that needed to happen. It was safe and easy for her daddy to bounce the ball, but for the fear to be conquered, Ava needed to do it.

After some time had passed, it also occurred to Ava that she was missing out on the full experience. Pausing from the running and giggling, she looked up at me with an outstretched arm and asked, "Daddy, can I try?"

This was the moment I had been hoping for. Like father, like daughter, Ava quickly slammed the bouncing ball against the concrete and soon we were running wildly and freely across the courtyard, chasing the ball and watching how high it could go. Ava needed to relearn to live fully, to press on to a place beyond the fear. She was only two, but this is true for each of us. The older we get and the more our bodies grow, fear finds ways to hide out in our soul. Ever more relentless to be heard, we must overcome fear and discover more of ourselves on the other side.

HOW HIGH CAN YOUR LIFE GO?

At some point, you have probably put your life in your pocket to keep it safe.

Maybe it was one big moment, but more than likely, it happened over several smaller moments. Somewhere along the way, fear made space in your heart. And that fear convinced you it was better to play it safe. Life was easier in the security of the pocket. It's too risky to love. It's too dangerous to dream. Hope is too costly. Only a few extraordinary people get to live remarkable lives. At times, you wonder if you're one of the few, but fear reminds you that you are not. In glimmers of exceptional moments, something sparks in your soul, and you imagine what it would be like to live a great story, chasing your God-given purpose. And as quickly as the glimmer rages like a wildfire in your soul, fear floods in and quenches the flame.

I know we haven't met, but can I share an important truth with you? Your life was not meant to be put in your pocket; it was meant to be fully lived. God made you with extraordinary purpose. You have great value. You are unlike any other. And if you can muster up the courage to offer your life back to God, He wants to show you how high it can go.

There may be moments where it feels like you're bouncing wildly out of control. There may be times when you feel lost against the dark L.A. sky. Don't lose heart. God is your good Father. He desires that you make a difference with your life even more than you do. If you'll keep offering your life back to God, He will ensure that you meet your destiny. You'll live fully and on purpose, overflowing with meaning.

Regardless of your age, of this I am sure: You have purpose. In order to lay hold of it, you will have to muster up the courage to press on. You'll inevitably encounter adversity. Don't run from the challenges. Your purpose is unearthed as you press on and push through. Don't let fear keep you from steps of faith. Don't let lies trip you up from laying hold of your purpose. Reach out and catch it. Learn to meet each day with a bounce perspective and a sense of childlike wonder. These become our best teachers.

THE JOURNEY BEGINS

We're taking this journey together. Do you desire to live fully? Are you willing to trust again? Will you take your life out of the security of your pocket and place it back in the artful hands of God?

If so, here's some really great news: God is a good Father. He's the Creator, and He made you with great purpose. As you submit your life to Him, He promises to do more through your life than you can imagine.

In order to lay hold of your purpose, you have to do what seems counterintuitive. You have to let go of it. You have to place it back into the hands of the One who saved it from bouncing out of control. At times, it will feel like it was just smashed against the concrete. You might misplace it at times against the dark night. Don't worry, He only wants to show you how high it can go.

QUESTIONS *for* TRANSFORMATION

1. If fear wasn't an option, how high can you imagine your life going?

2. Can you identify one or two key fears that have convinced you to play it safe?

3. As you look back on your life, can you see some moments when God might have rescued you when life was out of control?

4. What would it look like for you to trust God with more of your life?

5. Do you believe that God wants to show you how high your life can go? What's one step that you can take in order to let go and lay hold of it?

"You may not control all the events that happen to you, but you can decide not to be reduced by them."

—MAYA ANGELOU[3]

CHAPTER 2

CHANGE THE PLAYLIST

I can trick myself into thinking some pretty crazy things and I bet you can too. And when you live in a city like Los Angeles, you get used to seeing crazy things. The combination of these two—the ability to let your imagination run wild and living in a place where imagination comes to life—can often blur the lines of reality. At Disneyland, you'll ride next to famous athletes. While driving downtown, you'll see cameras hanging from cars, getting action shots for movies. You'll pick out your iPhone at the Apple Store with celebrities or ride on elevators with them at Ikea.

So, the morning that helicopters were chasing me in Downtown Pasadena, I knew it was about to get serious. But I'm getting a little ahead of myself. Let me back up for a moment to set the scene. Our apartment complex was comprised of several high-rise buildings, and one sat next to the 210 (freeway). So as not to muddy the beautiful mountain vistas, freeways drop below eyesight in Pasadena. And while I hadn't personally witnessed a high-speed car chase on the freeways, local morning news shows would often recount the spectacles from the prior day.

Most mornings, I'd go for a run in the city. Typically, I'd run south away from the freeway, then east along Colorado Boulevard (where they have the Rose Bowl Parade) and turn south down Lake Avenue. Early morning running required open eyes. Every now and then, my running would scare a person that had been sleeping on the street. They would hear me before I would see them. It would startle them, and then they would end up scaring me. While I loved these daybreak runs, I was vigilant while in the city. Eventually, I'd run out of downtown through the campus of Caltech and out to beautiful San Marino before running back.

On this particular morning, as I came back through Caltech's tree-lined campus, I could hear the familiar hum of several helicopters overhead, but I couldn't see them. I continued to run out of the campus and back onto Lake Avenue. As I reentered the city and looked up, I realized that there was a helicopter right above me, barely beyond the shop rooftops.

As I ran back up Lake Avenue toward our apartment, the helicopter moved north with me. This is when I began to feel a little nervous. *I've seen this play out on TV*, I thought. *There was probably a high-speed car chase on the 210, and now the offender has gone on foot.* Since the helicopter was continuing to hover over my head as I ran up Lake Avenue, I suspected that the person they were chasing would appear in front of me any second. I picked up my pace and ran with my fists clinched, ready to fight. If I was going to come face-to-face with a fugitive and be on TV screens across L.A., I was going to be the hero. This fool was going down.

Eventually, I made my way back to Colorado Boulevard. Now I no longer saw just one helicopter overhead, but at least four circling above me. As I ran west onto Colorado, now sprinting to make it back to the apartment, the first helicopter stayed in place, and another began to track with me.

This is when it dawned on me, *Not only are these helicopters chasing down a bad guy, they think I'm the bad guy.* I wasn't prepared for this moment. It was beginning to feel like I was caught up in the filming of an action-packed blockbuster. *So this is what it's like to be Jason Bourne*, I thought. I was either the next action star or a felon on the run. Soon, police cars were going to encircle me and FBI agents would rappel out of the helicopters.

Now running as fast as I could down Colorado Boulevard, I reached Madison Avenue and sprinted north. Our apartment complex was just two blocks away. *Surely I can make it,* I hoped. And then, the most epic thing happened. As I approached the steps to our apartment complex, a helicopter lifted straight up and emerged above the apartment building that set up against the 210 and then headed straight toward me.

This is it, I thought. *This is when they take me out.*

Skipping every other step, I ran up the steps to our building, dashed inside, and unlocked our door. Out of breath, heart racing, blood pumping, and legs weak, I tried to tell Katie what was going on. "You're not—going to believe—what's happening outside," I wheezed.

"I know!" Katie exclaimed. "There was a really bad wreck on the 210 freeway, just on the other side of the apartment complex. It seems like every news helicopter in L.A. is hovering over Pasadena watching it. In fact, someone is badly injured, and a medevac helicopter just airlifted them off the freeway to take them to the hospital."

Still catching my breath, I blurted out, "I know! That's exactly what I thought was going on!" Of course, I was far too embarrassed to tell her what I really believed.

I had completely made up a story in my mind. Although it was a grand story and everything I saw actually happened, the reality I had constructed was completely false.

Our imaginations can narrate some pretty fantastic stories. I made up that story based on what I could see and perceive, and you can sometimes make up stories too. The reality we construct is often false. Imaginations are consistent across ages, genders, and ethnicities. They often sound like,

"No one likes me . . ." "Everyone else has it easier than I do . . ." "I'm never going to get ahead . . ." "I don't have what it takes . . ." "I cannot overcome the events of my life . . ."

It is critically important we understand that most of us believe some form of the same three lies: "I'm unloved," "I'm unapproved," and, "I'm unacceptable." Each of us believe one of them more than the other, but most believe all three to some level. But this must be learned too: Not a single one of them is true.

SO LOVED

If you're going to lay hold of the secrets to living fully, it will not be absent of a deep sense of immense worth. Specifically, it will be realizing that the God of the universe made you out of love. From the core of your being, you must come to a fuller recognition that the One who made you is crazy about you.

Most people grow up thinking that God is mad at them. I have three theological degrees and I've thoroughly studied the Bible for over twenty years. Here's my grand conclusion: You are *so incredibly loved*. I know that God isn't angry or disappointed with you. How do I know this? I know what God did for you.

You probably know John 3:16—"For God *so loved* the world that he gave his one and only Son, that whoever believes in him shall not perish but have eternal life" (NIV, emphasis added). You are *so loved*. God is over the moon about you. God can't stop thinking about you.

I recently bought a new iPhone and as I paid for it, I thought, *I can't believe I'm spending this much on a phone.* But it was worth it. How do I know this? Because I paid dearly for it. You are *so loved* that God would buy your life with the price of His only Son. To think less is to think less of God's sacrifice. To really truly live fully, you must grow in your belief that the Creator designed you out of love. You aren't one among billions to God. You are distinct and worth the life of His one and only Son.

APPROVED AND SET APART

There's probably a good chance that for far too long, you've believed the lie that you don't have a purpose. Or perhaps you believe that people are made with purpose, but for whatever reason, you'll never accomplish yours. However, each of us innately feels something that pulls us forward, wooing us to a greater destiny. This isn't an accident, and this isn't unique to you. God had something that He wanted to bring about in the world, so He made you.

Some people feel that drive so deeply and yet, at the same time, they feel overlooked and pushed aside. Therefore, they'll do whatever it takes for others to notice and approve of them. Of course, this can go in dangerous directions. One might become a workaholic, spending far too much time at the office, neglecting those that love them and already approve of them. Another may find approval within a gym or fitness setting. This can seem healthy, but only the individual can know their intent. If it is to have others boost their esteem, this road has no end. Others may date person after person, seeking someone who will adequately admire them. Even pastors can easily fall prey to this unhealthy mindset and wrongly believe they only have worth when on a stage communicating to a crowd.

The following truth is crucial to lock into your spirit, so please dial in with me for a moment: You are already approved by the Creator who made you. You don't have to live *for* the approval of others because you can live *from* the approval of God. You don't have to prove your worth; God already affirmed your worth when He asked His only Son Jesus to die in your place. You are deeply loved and made with divine purpose. Every day, you can wake up and live *from* a place of affection and approval, which means you don't have to go searching for them. You already have them. So, you can live to love others and live out your God-given purpose.

And this is why I love the Bible so profoundly. We learn powerful truths like this: If you are a follower of Jesus, all of the promises that God has ever spoken become your birthright (2 Corinthians 1:20). That's right—*every* promise of God is given to you. Consider God's words over the life of Jeremiah: "'Before I formed you in the womb I knew you, before you were born I set you apart;'" (Jeremiah 1:5 NIV). This becomes true of you.

God knows and loves you. God set you apart to bring about a purpose on this earth. You don't have to prove it to anyone. You get to walk in God's confidence knowing that as His child, you are loved and approved. And if you ever feel that you'll never accomplish your purpose, remember that since God made you on purpose, He is zealous for your purpose to come about. God is even more inclined for you to live into your destiny than you are. It's why the psalmist declares, "The Lord will fulfill his purpose for me . . ." (Psalm 138:8).

ACCEPTED TO ACCEPT

So often, many people never live into their divine purpose because they devote so much time believing lies about their worth. In essence, most people never fully see the kind of impact they could make on those around them because they aren't convinced that *they* are valuable. So, instead of spending their days making others feel accepted, they are desperately trying to get others to accept them.

So much of life feels like we are all bouncing around in a pinball machine, bumping into and zooming past each other so fast that we never really see one another. One person may not feel accepted widely so they try to find comfort in one or two individuals. So as not to disrupt their safe space, they exclude others so that they won't be excluded. If you look up and scan what's happening around you, this is so much of what we see around us at work, at school, and in our community. People just want to be accepted, but it usually comes at the expense of others being excluded.

That's not God's plan for our lives. Consider the words of the Apostle Paul: "Therefore, accept each other just as Christ has accepted you so that God will be given glory" (Romans 15:7 NLT). When Jesus is your Lord, Paul says you are already accepted by God. You don't have to prove it, earn it, or justify it. Regardless of how many followers you have on social media, irrespective to your accomplishments, and unrelated to the size of your bank account, you are accepted by God.

So, just as you are accepted by God, Paul challenges us to go and accept others. Imagine how different your life would be if instead of living *for* the acceptance of others, you lived *from* the acceptance of God. Then, because you are fully accepted, you can spend your days helping others know their value and worth.

CHANGE THE PLAYLIST

I listen to music so much that it's almost hard to imagine a time before popular apps like Spotify, Apple Music, and Amazon Music. I can still remember simultaneously holding down the play and record button on my boombox to make mixtapes while listening to the radio. Those were good times, but nothing beats the ease of creating a playlist on your phone.

What's more, I often find these playlists to be lifesavers, especially when our kids were much younger. During long road trips when attitudes were turning sour, the noise was growing louder, and perhaps the winding road was creating nausea, I discovered that my playlists were quite powerful. If the kids were irritable, I'd turned on some jazz from greats like John Coltrane, Herbie Hancock, and my favorite—Preservation Hall Jazz Band. Or, if the kids were fighting over media devices and it was summertime, I'd roll down the windows and play my road trip playlist with musicians like James Taylor, Chris Stapleton, and Darius Rucker. If I needed to lighten the mood, we might sing aloud to Ed Sheeran, Johnnyswim, or some classics like Ben E. King or Sam Cooke. However, as the kids grow older, and especially as we are driving to school, I'll turn on worship playlists so that the kids are reminded of how great God is and how deeply they are loved. As the situation demands, I'll change the playlist.

Let me suggest something for you. When you find yourself believing the lies that you are unloved, unapproved, and unaccepted, change the playlist. I don't simply mean that you should change your song selection, though that may be helpful. Beyond the music you play, you need to change the playlist of the thoughts that swirl in your soul. In the Bible, Peter knew what it was like to endeavor to pursue God fully while also dealing with a broken past. However, as he matured in Christ, he understood the importance of laying hold of the truth that in Christ, he was a new creation: "But you are a chosen people, a royal priesthood, a holy nation, God's special possession, that you may declare the praises of him who called you out of darkness into his wonderful light" (1 Peter 2:9 NIV).

What Peter declared to the church is true of you today as a follower of Jesus! You are chosen, which means God selected you out of love (Deuteronomy 7:7-8). You are royal, a minister before God and a child of the king. God is using your life to conduct His Kingdom work (1 Peter 2:5). Everything that God says about Jesus becomes true of you. You are an heir of God, a co-heir with Christ (Romans 8:17), which means you are set apart to God regardless of your faults and failures (1 Corinthians 1:2).

Peter said that you are "God's special possession." Take that in for a moment; you belong to God. Full stop. God called you by name, and you are His. Nothing can overcome you, and you are never alone. You are precious to God, honorable and lovely. If you find yourself thinking anything else, change the playlist.

DECLARE IT

You are loved, approved, and accepted by the Creator of the universe, not because you've earned it but simply because you are a child of the King. This is great news. If you didn't earn it, you can't lose it. And if you can't lose it, you don't have to keep being good enough to retain it. Each and every day, you can live who you are because of your standing before God. Which means that instead of trying to find love, approval, and acceptance, you can live out your God-given purpose to help others feel loved, approved, and accepted. And this is when life begins to get interesting.

However, I must caution you: This kind of mindset must be fought for. You and I can have as many as sixty thousand thoughts in a day. This fact alone is somewhat exhausting. Add to this that science has learned that eighty percent of these thoughts can be negative.[4] We simply cannot have a positive life when we're consumed with such negative thoughts. In order to live out our purposes, we'll have to daily retrain our brains to believe what's true. We'll literally have to rewire our brains, and it is possible.

I do this by writing and speaking daily declarations over my life. These are biblical truths that combat the lies I'm tempted to believe. They help me demolish negative and untruthful ways of thinking, and they aid me in establishing a positive and truthful mindset. Our lives advance in the path of our thoughts. What begins as a thought works out in actions, and our actions add up to our life experience. So, if I want to live into my God-given purpose, I'll have to start with believing it. I'll have to retrain my brain to believe that I am deeply loved. I'll have to wholly realize that I'm approved. In order to help others feel accepted, I'll have to put in the work to instruct my soul on my own acceptance.[5]

I regularly remind myself of biblical truths through declarations. On my own, I don't have what it takes, but in God, I am more than enough for every task, challenge, and opportunity (Exodus 3:11-12). I am chosen and loved, a son to the King, and a warrior of the Most High God (1 Peter 2:9). My identity is in Jesus, not my successes nor my failures. I am loved because I am a son (1 John 3:1). I have more than enough energy, wisdom, and resources to accomplish my calling (Ephesians 2:10). So, I have purpose and meaning because I am creative and anointed (Psalm 139:13-16). Declarations like these remind me that I am not overcome by lies and negativity because the Overcomer lives in me (Romans 8:37)!

PUT IT ALL TOGETHER

The beautiful truth that you'll come to realize is this: Your destiny is not somewhere in the future, waiting for your arrival. Rather, when you embody the truths that you are loved, approved, and accepted, you can live out your destiny today. Sure, you will get better over time. You'll uncover more about your unique purpose and you'll discover more opportunities to bring those distinctives to life. With the mindfulness from this book, you'll experience greater impact and fulfillment. Every day can have deep meaning. Each experience can be full of God-given purpose and destiny. Best of all, it can all start *today.*

Let the people around you experience your wholeness. Begin to imagine the influence you can have as you live hopeful and as you help others feel unconditional love, approval, and acceptance. The world will be better because you served a higher purpose—not just some day in the future but today!

QUESTIONS for TRANSFORMATION

1. Which of the three lies (I'm unloved; I'm unapproved; and I'm unaccepted) have you believed the most?

2. How has negative and untruthful thinking held you back from believing God's best for your life?

3. In what ways could you experience transformation if you began to believe that you are *so loved* by God? (John 3:16)

4. If you're ready to "change the playlist," what truths do you need to declare about your life?

"Security is mostly a superstition . . . Avoiding danger is no safer in the long run than outright exposure . . . Faith alone defends. Life is either a daring adventure or nothing."

—HELEN KELLER[6]

CHAPTER 3

THROW YOURSELF INTO THE SEA

"How did this happen? I was only fishing."

Peter must have felt a great deal of pain, fear, and confusion. He probably muttered to himself, "I was literally minding my own business, doing my thing. Then Jesus invited me, an *uneducated man*, to follow him."

Like most young men, Peter had gone into the family business. Following in the footsteps of rabbis? That was for the distinguished and learned, not grunt workers like Peter. And yet, Jesus invited him to leave his nets made of rope and begin casting spiritual nets to fish for people. Peter was in the midst of a great adventure and living his greatest story, but then it all came crashing down.

I can only guess at the depth of hurt that Peter must have felt. Even so, his story resonates profoundly with me. The longer I have followed God, the greater the risks I've taken, and the greater the disappointments I've experienced. Just like Peter, you and I will have moments when it seems like disappointment overtakes us. However, we must learn that obstacles aren't the end of the story. The best part is just around the corner. Peter had thrown in the towel, believing he didn't have what it takes. What happened next changed everything.

For three and a half years, Peter witnessed people being healed in front of his eyes. He was there when thousands of people crowded mountainsides to hear Jesus speak. Not only was he in the boat when the wind and sea submitted to the voice of Jesus, but Peter himself briefly walked on the water. Peter wasn't *kind of* following Jesus; he didn't have one foot in and one foot out. When he first began following Jesus, everyone knew him as Simon the fisherman. Now, he was Peter, the rock, the Christ follower. Peter was all-in. There was no turning back.

One night, all the disciples were sitting with Jesus eating the Passover meal together. Jesus predicted that he would be betrayed by one of them. Peter declared, "I will never leave you!" But then the plot twisted. Jesus was betrayed by Judas and handed over to authorities. As Peter followed closely, people began to notice him. He had, of course, been at the right hand of Jesus those several years as the crowds had flocked to hear that great prophet.

As Peter sat around a fire, a young girl asked if he knew Jesus. Full of fear, Peter began cussing at the girl as he denied Jesus. (Remember when I said that people in the Bible are far from perfect?) Two more times, he was noticed, and each time, Peter declared emphatically, "I don't know the man!"

In custody, not far away, Jesus's eyes meet Peter's.

How did I fall so far so fast? Peter must have bitterly thought. *Only hours ago, I forcefully asserted my allegiance, and just now I cowardly distanced myself from my Lord.*

Soon, Jesus was brutally beaten, mocked, and shamefully hung on a cross. In time, he was barely recognizable as a human. The sky turned black, the earth shook, and Jesus was placed in a borrowed tomb.

GONE FISHING

For three days, Peter's emotions overwhelmed him. He shifted from guilt to confusion, and then on to grief and fear. Finally, Peter couldn't take it anymore. He quit. He told the other disciples, "I'm going out to fish" (John 21:3 NIV). Peter wasn't going out for lunch. Peter was going back to his old way of living.

Just like Ava put the bouncing ball in her pocket to keep it safe, Peter decided that following Jesus was much too risky and just too hard. He was putting his life back in his pocket to play it safe. Peter was going *back* to fishing, *back* to when life was easier, even if that also meant less purposeful.

In *The Problem of Pain,* C.S. Lewis writes, "It is natural for us to wish that God had designed for us a less glorious and less arduous destiny; but then *we are wishing not for more love but for less*" (emphasis added).[7] Think about the last major goal you accomplished. Almost certainly there were moments of discomfort, even pain, in that journey. The bigger your goal, the more likely you are to encounter struggle along the way. But consider the implications of Lewis's statement: God loves you so much and *trusts* you to grow into your purpose.

I've been following Jesus now for more than a quarter of a century, and sadly, I've seen person after person make the same decision never to return (or at least not with the same vitality). When Jesus told the disciples that following Him would mean they'd have to take up their own cross, He wasn't playing around. Following Jesus is not for the faint of heart. Following a man that willingly laid down His life under the most brutal circumstances imaginable does not equate to a safe and predictable life. Following Jesus will stretch you beyond your human capacities, and it isn't safe by any means, but it will cause you to lay hold of your divine purpose. And as we'll learn from Peter in this story, there's absolutely nothing that compares to following Jesus with reckless abandon.

CRUCIBLE SEASONS

Interestingly, just as Peter threw in the towel, Jesus showed up on the scene. In fact, that became the *third* time the disciples encountered Jesus *after* His resurrection (John 21:14). The *third* time. Not once, but two other times before this moment, these disciples had met with the risen Lord. On the first occasion, Jesus appeared to them as they hid in fear behind locked doors (John 20:19). Then, eight days later, Jesus again walked through locked doors and convinced the still-doubting Thomas (John 20:26).

And yet, after all of this, Peter went back to fishing. In John 21, Peter and the other fishermen worked all night and caught nothing. Early the next morning, Jesus appeared and called from the shore, "Have you caught any fish?"

They didn't recognize Him, but surely this question added insult to injury.

"Throw the nets on the other side of the boat," Jesus suggested.

If we're reading with fresh eyes, this part of the story is laughable. If we too had been in that boat all night, I'm guessing we would have already tried this not-so-innovative maneuver. Jesus wasn't offering them state-of-the-art fishing techniques, as though "the other side of the boat" was such a better fishing spot than the original side of the boat. That wasn't the point. Jesus was inviting the disciples, and Peter especially, into a divine moment. After a crushing setback, Peter had retreated to the safety of familiarity . . . only to find more disappointment. But at Peter's lowest moment, Jesus seized the opportunity to move Peter forward.

Learn from this story. There are times when it feels like our faith may be crumbling, and simultaneously it can feel like our faith has never been stronger. We feel that one second, we know nothing, and the next one, we feel like heaven has never been closer. As I look back on my own life, these seasons are too numerous to fully recount. There have been periods of prolonged waiting, painful times of grief and confusion, and seasons when my faith was stretched far beyond my limited capacity to comprehend. But God allows these seasons to stretch and grow us into the person He wants to develop.

These are crucible seasons, and God knows that in them, we need Him even more than before. These seasons are priceless for spiritual enrichment and for growing closer to God. Don't run away from God in these seasons; do whatever you can to cling to Him. In time, you'll discover your faith has enlarged and your relationship with God has blossomed.

FAITH AND FEAR: THROW YOURSELF INTO THE SEA

Soon, the disciples pulled in a large number of fish—perhaps their greatest catch ever. That's when John realized that it was Jesus on the shore. Upon learning this, Peter put on his outer garment and threw himself into the sea. I love this, and I love learning from Peter. As Peter grew as a follower of Jesus, he learned to bring his head alongside his heart. And yet, I think God is often pleased when our hearts go first. Peter wasn't thinking rationally, and he wasn't considering all the options. He just wanted to get close to Jesus. Instead of riding the boat to the shore, Peter jumped out and swam one hundred yards. Most of us would prefer not to run the length of a football field, let alone swim one—especially when we were inhabiting a perfectly functional boat. None of that mattered to Peter. He threw himself into the sea. He didn't care about the large catch of fish. He didn't care about the nets and the boats. Peter had left them before, and he was choosing to leave them again. Why? Peter just wanted to get to Jesus.

Earlier, Peter had declared that he was going back to a life of fishing. But this miraculous catch had reminded Peter of what it is like to follow after the Son of God. Moreover, it reminded him that once you've walked in the presence of Jesus, any other way of life is found wanting. Peter was in a crucible season. Yes, it was easier to play it safe, but playing it safe would not get him to his destiny. Playing it safe will not lead us to live our greatest stories.

Why had Peter gone back to fishing? Fear had begun to make a home in his heart. Just like Ava was afraid to lose her bouncing ball, Peter was afraid of losing everything—his hopes, his dreams, and his expectations. Fishing was his security blanket. When the rest of his world was crumbling, fishing made sense. Yet, on this particular night, even fishing didn't come easy. If Jesus could make the fish appear on the other side of the boat, Jesus could also make the fish stay away all night long. Peter knew this to be true. He had seen Jesus bend natural laws to create moments for others. This was Peter's moment, and he wasn't going to let it pass him by. He would have swum from the middle of the sea if it meant getting in the presence of Jesus.

Quite often, this is the most important thing that you can do. Do whatever it takes to get in the presence of Jesus. Throw yourself into the sea. Swim a hundred yards. Just get to Jesus. Fear had kept Peter away; faith was pulling him back. For all the things Peter got wrong in the gospel narrative, he got this right. This is why Peter is the masterclass teacher on faith.

Whether you consider yourself a follower of Jesus or not, my encouragement to you is to do whatever it takes to get in the presence of Jesus. Pursuing Jesus is a bit like wearing glasses for the first time. His presence brings your life into focus, and paradoxically you learn to take comfort in His presence, even in the thick of uncertainty. It's like knowing that behind the storm clouds, the sun still shines brightly. If you're not a follower of Jesus, I invite you to walk with Jesus too. Reach out to a friend or family member that you respect. Visit a life-giving church nearby. Reach out to our church, and we'll do our best to help you find a group of people near you who can be a safe place for you to explore faith. If you're already a follower of Jesus, it's time to jump back into the water. God is using this book to beckon you back. Don't be satisfied with a head knowledge of Jesus; pursue a heart passion for God's presence. I promise you God has more waiting for you, but you won't find it sitting in the boat.

GETTING PAST YOUR PAST

We should never confuse repentance and conviction with shame and disappointment. God loves you beyond your comprehension. God *will* convict you of sin in order to lead you to His best. God will teach you repentance so that you can leave that sin behind, which will free you to the life you were made to live. But you can't step into your future until you move past your past. Once you place your past into the grace-filled hands of God, every time your old life tries to remind you of your history, you get to remind it of God's grace and restoration. The old has gone and the new has come.

Back on the shore, the disciples hauled in the big catch—153 fish in all. Leave it to fishermen to count every single one. When they had finished gawking at the fish, they noticed that Jesus had prepared a fire so they could share a meal together. Here again, they had just witnessed Jesus' power over the natural world. And what was Jesus interested in? Jesus wanted to spend time with them.

As the fire's glow gave way to the morning sun, Jesus and Peter had some unfinished business to deal with, but not in the way that you might imagine. If you and I were Jesus, we'd want to talk with Peter about how he abandoned us in our time of greatest need. We'd point out how his arrogance at the Last Supper gave way to cowardice on the way to the cross. But Jesus isn't like us. Jesus is full of truth and grace. The truth needed to be dealt with, but grace would shower the conversation with the compassion of God.

"Do you love me more than these?" Jesus asked Peter while pointing to the fish. Perhaps Peter was taken off guard by the question; of *course* he loved Jesus more than fish. And yet, he had gone back to fishing.

"Yes, Lord! You know I love you."

Then Jesus asked Peter again, "Do you love me?"

Undoubtedly, Peter's emotions and thoughts were stirring within himself. *I do love Jesus, and yet, I left Jesus.* Then, a third time Jesus asked, "Peter, do you love me?"

Peter was so grieved by the questioning, but every time, he gave his most authentic answer: "Yes, of course I love you."

While Jesus asked three seemingly identical questions, He was after three different objectives. First, He sought redemption and restoration for Peter. In front of crowds, Peter had denied Jesus three times. Now, in front of the disciples, Jesus gave Peter the opportunity to declare his devotion three times. Jesus was redeeming Peter's greatest moment of guilt and shame, and He was restoring Peter to full fellowship with his closest community.

Jesus isn't shocked when we falter. Rather, God knows better than us how sin wrecks our lives. While it might shock us, God isn't surprised by the lengths that sin will take us. When you come to grips with this fact, you'll be able to receive grace into your life and to extend it with generosity to the people around you.

While God is not surprised by our sin, God also desires to separate us from that sin. Peter was overcome with guilt and shame. Fear *and regret* caused him to go back to fishing. Simply put, he couldn't get past his past. Peter couldn't conceive of a future full of faith and impact because his past kept him in a place of humiliation and weakness. Jesus didn't ask him to declare his allegiance because Jesus wanted to know where Peter stood. Jesus knew full well the depths of Peter's love, and He wanted to give him the opportunity to reaffirm it. In declaring his love for the Son of God, Peter was given a road to restoration . . . and to wisdom.

WHEN PASSION AND WISDOM MEET

Jesus' second objective for Peter was to grow his wisdom to the level of his passion. In the English language, we have only one word for love. This often leaves us anemic when trying to express nuance in affection. We say we love our family or friends, and in the next sentence, we express our love for tacos. I do love tacos—and cake and coffee. But as much as I appreciate those things, they are but a shadow of how much love I feel for my wife and kids.

When Jesus asked Peter the first time, "Do you love me?" He used the term *agape* for love. In the Greek language, *agape* is the highest form of love. *Agape* love is unconditional, a divine love that goes beyond feeling to sacrificial action. But when Peter said, "Yes, Lord, you know that I love you," he didn't respond with *agape*. He said, "Yes, Lord, you know that I *phileo* you." *Phileo*, as you might guess from Philadelphia (the City of Brotherly Love), is love most seen in a warm friendship.

Then, the second time Jesus asked Peter, He again said, "Do you have *agape* love for me?" Again, Peter responded, "Yes, Lord, I have *phileo* love for you." Once you understand this, the scene becomes a little comical, as though the two of them aren't having the same conversation. It seems like the old Abbott and Costello routine, "Who's on First?" And yet, something powerful is taking place.

When Jesus asked Peter the third time, "Do you love me?" He used the word *phileo*. Peter responded, "Yes, Lord, I have a *phileo* love for you." At first glance, it can appear that Jesus had conceded to Peter. However, something more profound was happening: Jesus met Peter *where he was.*

When Jesus asked, "Peter, do you still claim to have a divine love for Me?"

Peter responded in humility, "Jesus, I don't yet know how to love like that, but I do love you like a brother. I do love You with all the love that I know and understand." And that's all that God asks of us. "With where you are right now, with what you know today, will you love Me?"

Wisdom begins when God meets us where we are. As we grow toward maturity, we can rest assured that God is with us every step of the way. We aren't alone, nor do we have to struggle under the belief that we are reaching for a God who is far away.

Don't let what you have yet to learn prevent you from moving forward. You'll never feel like you've arrived. Arrival isn't the destination; living fully every day is the objective. This will take daily passion while continuing to mature in wisdom.

YOU, FOLLOW ME

If we ever think that following God is reserved for those pursuing a safe and unadventurous life, the final exchange in John 21 should put that to rest. Peter would get the chance to demonstrate his commitment to Christ with his very life. And this was the third objective Jesus was accomplishing with His three questions. In essence, "Peter, are you sure you want to follow me? It will cost you everything, even your life."

This isn't reserved for Peter alone. Our lives are not our own. And this is the crux of this book. Since God made you to live, your greatest gift back to God is living most fully. You aren't made to just get by. You aren't designed to play it safe. You are made to live—designed to worship the Creator with your whole life.

Jesus forecasted how Peter would pay the ultimate price. Just like Jesus, he would be crucified. We can easily forgive Peter if the shock and trauma of the past few days flooded back into his soul, even with all the miraculous moments of this unforgettable morning. In fact, I'd say Peter's response is a forerunner of how most of us see our lives and calling. As soon as Jesus spoke, Peter turned to John and brazenly asked, "What about him?"

Jesus nips that conversation firmly in the bud. "If I want him to remain alive, what is that to you? *You* follow me" (John 21:22 NIV, emphasis added).

Jesus was forcefully asserting to Peter that while he's not the main character, he is at the center of the story. Jesus may be the protagonist, but Peter (and each of us) has a key part to play.

But most of us don't want to play *our* part; we want to play somebody else's role. We think they get all the breaks. Things just fall into place for them. Clearly there is a bit of a rivalry between John and Peter, but in John's defense, only one disciple stood at the foot of the cross. John held Jesus's mother while she witnessed her son's brutal murder. Everyone wants to be called "the disciple whom Jesus loved," but not everyone shows up for the moments that matter. We all want someone else's story, but not everyone is willing to pay their price. Before you covet another's journey, learn the sacrifices they've made.

In effect, Jesus was saying, "Peter, I'm talking to *you*. *You* must follow me." Peter could not live his life to the fullest if he was trying to fill someone else's shoes. He had to live *his* story to the fullest. And the same is true for you.

Of course, we can and should learn from others, especially from those who live fully. But we can't live their lives because we're made to live our own. Jesus tells us, "I want to show you how high *your* life can go. Stop believing the lie that I made someone else with more purpose. I made *you* with great purpose. You, *you* must follow Me."

And follow we must. There is no cookie-cutter approach to following Jesus because He didn't create you with a template or mold. He uniquely designed and fashioned you with distinct passions, personality, and plans.

Learning to follow Him will come from daily pursuit. As you continue in the subsequent chapters, I will be your coach and running partner. You can do this.

QUESTIONS *for* TRANSFORMATION

1. How have past challenges caused you to play it safe with your future?

2. Are you currently in a crucible season? How will this fuel you to follow God with renewed passion?

3. Do you need to let God restore past brokenness? How could this free you to follow God with your future?

4. How have you allowed comparison to hold you back from living your greatest story? From this point forward, how will you follow Jesus fully and uniquely?

ATTRIBUTE 2
MADE to ACT

Reverse Weariness, Crush Inaction, Eradicate Escape

"A faith that does not do things is a dead faith."
—James 2:17 NLV

"Let me tell you the secret which has led me to the goal. My only strength resides in my tenacity."

—LOUIS PASTEUR[8]

CHAPTER 4

KEEP ON DRIVING

On Moving Day, we were hopelessly stuck in the driveway.

We'd just sold the home we renovated—a nineteenth-century bungalow in a historical neighborhood of Terre Haute, Indiana. We were about to set our course for Pasadena, California. On the surface, our plan seemed completely irrational. We would be leaving everything we knew and loved. Even so, my amazing bride, Katie, and I believed that God was inviting us to reach out and catch our purpose. We had to leave a lot behind in order to move toward our dreams.

But now it seemed we wouldn't be moving at all.

I had spent all day loading the trailer, placing all the heavy furniture in the front, then adding boxes and miscellaneous items. And this is probably a great place for a confession: I knew nothing about packing a trailer, and I had zero experience hauling a trailer two thousand miles across the country. I backed up my Nissan Xterra, connected the trailer, and attempted to remove the block beneath the trailer's hitch.

The block wouldn't budge.

I borrowed a sledgehammer from a neighbor and began pounding the block. Our idyllic departure from the house was suddenly overshadowed by my ignorance. I gave one final swing, the block flew out, and the front of the trailer rushed toward the ground. The trailer and Xterra were connected in the shape of a V, with the front of our car hanging high in the air.

I had foolishly placed all the weight in the front of the trailer instead of balancing it over the single axel. Over the next several hours, my family patiently helped us unload everything on the trailer, and then meticulously reload it as the sun set on the first day of our adventure.

As you run after God's best for your life, you will make mistakes, and there will be setbacks. Before we had even hit the road, I made a big error, and I was so embarrassed. It makes me wonder how many people stop chasing their God-given dreams because they stumble out of the gates. Just like family that came to our side, we need to trust that God will place people in our corner who graciously open our eyes and keep us moving forward.

There are days when it will seem like the universe is conspiring for our good, but there will also be days when it feels like the whole world is against us. Both are real. In John 10:10, Jesus made this clear: "'The thief comes only to steal and kill and destroy; I have come that they may have life, and have it to the full'" (NIV). There is a thief that desires to take you out, move you off course, and distract you from your purpose. But take heart: The thief is no match for the Giver of Life. There are going to be some bumps in the road. Keep driving.

DON'T STOP IN NEEDLES

Since we had a toddler, we reasoned that early morning driving would help Ava sleep. Just one problem: We didn't consider that most gas stations would be closed. We had barely crossed into Illinois and the weight of the trailer was rapidly draining our gas tank. We pulled off at exit after exit, looking for an open gas station before finally finding one just before the tank emptied.

For the next three days, we could watch our gas gauge move toward "E" as we drove down Interstate 40 toward California. We were once so low on gas that I popped the vehicle in neutral and we coasted down a New Mexico mountainside in the middle of the desert, praying there would be a gas station at the valley floor. There was! I also recall that as we slowly climbed out of the valley in Albuquerque, an oversized semi-trailer passed us like we were standing still.

Unfortunately, it wasn't until later in the trip that I finally realized you can't haul a fourteen-foot trailer with an Xterra. Soon, we were in Kingman, Arizona, and our small SUV was not doing well. Not only were we were stopping for gas every hour, but now the air conditioning had stopped working. Did I mention that we moved in early July, and we were now heading into the Mojave Desert? Thinking that I had completely failed my young family, I pulled off the interstate and parked in a slightly shady spot beneath a parched pine tree. *What was I thinking?* I kept asking myself. But it was far too late to turn back, and Kingman was not our destination, so we kept on driving.

Temperatures neared 120 degrees, we had no air conditioning, and the car was beginning to overheat. We pulled into a gas station, parked under an awning for some shade, and sat inside a Burger King to get cooled off. Things were getting worse, and I was fearful that we'd soon be stranded. There was a town with hotels just across the California border. I was praying with my whole being that we could make it.

As we crossed the Colorado River into our new home state, things went from awful to insufferable. We pulled up to a border crossing inspection site, and for two kids from Indiana, it felt like entering a foreign country. Now fully saturated with sweat, we sat in the hot sun awaiting our turn.

Soon an agent approached our vehicle, looked in the back of our car, and said, "Sir, do you realize that your daughter is not doing well?" *This is it,* I thought. *This is the end of the line. He's going to arrest me for child neglect.* "Yes," I replied, "and if you'll let us through, I'm trying to get to a hotel at the exit." He asked me to open the trailer for inspection. I told him it was loaded down and opening it might invoke an avalanche. He persisted. I slowly opened the door, he took a quick peek, and with great mercy said, "Welcome to California."

We arrived in the sun-scorched city of Needles, California. If you're wondering whether you should visit, let me spare you the trouble. Needles is exactly as it sounds—maybe even worse than it sounds. We found what I presumed was the cleanest hotel in town. Outside it was 120 degrees, and the hotel lobby was marginally better. We ascended the steps of the motel with our luggage, entered our room, turned on the air conditioner, and fell onto the beds. We soon realized that the A/C unit didn't work and asked for a new room. The air conditioning unit in the new room *sort of* worked. In order to cool off, we decided to go the hotel pool. We jumped in, hopeful that this would lift our spirits. It didn't. The water was green, hot, and had a funny smell. We hit the showers *fast.*

We desperately needed sleep. Just before turning out the lights, I noticed something strange on a wall. As I looked closer, I noticed little green worms climbing out of a tiny hole. I was on the brink of a literal and figurative meltdown. Unable to sleep, I closely monitored the temperature outside. When we got back into the Xterra at three a.m., it was a refreshing 110 degrees. We were only four hours from our destination; it was time to get the heck out of hell.

Finally, three and a half days after my trailer mishap, we arrived in Pasadena. I suspect that with no A/C, windows down, and an overheated car, we looked less like the Fresh Prince arriving in Bel Air and more like the Beverly Hillbillies. Though in the same state, Pasadena is to Needles as filet mignon is to roadkill.

Imagine with me for a moment that I could get in the mind of my toddler inside that motel. What if Ava was thinking something like *Dad, what have you done? It's hot outside. The car's not working. And it's better inside the hotel. Let's just stay here.* Obviously from my vantage point, that would be crazy. I knew what was coming down the road. However, many people stop way short of God's best. While chasing down their God-given dreams, many people encounter several roadblocks. They face one detour after another. Instead of moving forward, they stop in Needles. It feels easier to face the familiarity of the current misery than to guess at the unknown future.

Sometimes the most spiritual thing that you can do is keep driving. You haven't come this far to stop in Needles. Some people never reach their destiny simply because they give up too soon. God's best will never be easy. God's best will be more about the character developed within you than it will be about the external, visible markers of success.

Character is forged in the fire. Deep-won character is more important than a job promotion. Character that's been fortified through trial is worth far more than a pay raise. Greater than the new house or the next car, character qualities like perseverance and tenacity will make it possible for God to bring greater impact through your life. Don't run from the roadblocks. Don't flee from the detours. And by all means, don't stop in Needles. Just keep driving.

MARCH SEVEN TIMES

In Joshua 6, the nation of Israel was given one of the worst military strategies ever. Think about it for a moment. Instead of invading the city by surprise, God told the whole army to march around the city. Now, the city was fully alert that an opposing force was soon to attack. Moreover, the people of Jericho got full view of every person, a complete head count, with plenty of time for a scouting report. They were to do this not one time but *daily* for *six days*. This timeframe allowed the Jericho defenses to fortify their territory, to re-position, and to develop a counter-attack—not to mention ample time for their own army to get in some naps.

Then, on the seventh day, they do the whole march-around seven more times. Just in case the people of Jericho needed warning that this whole thing was intensifying, now they knew! These marchers were really serious. And just to prove it, they'd march until their legs felt like jelly, until their shoulders could no longer carry the weight of their armor, until their lungs screamed. That'll show them! And, oh yeah, when it was time to really fight, they'd blow the trumpets and shout loudly just to make sure that Jericho was ready.

From a strategic viewpoint, this was a terrible plan. But God doesn't need a strategy. God isn't opposed to good strategies and good planning either. It's just that God's favor out-maneuvers the best strategy every time. One moment, one breath, one touch from God completely turns the tables of power.

The marching didn't have much to do with the people of Jericho, but it had everything to do with the people of Israel. Would they obey God? Moreover, would they obey God's directives fully? Would they get partial credit if they stopped on the third day and decided to blow the trumpets? What if they stopped on six? Let's say that on the seventh day, on the sixth time around, they saw Jericho preparing to fire at will. Would they have marched one more rotation? God said to march for seven days, and on the seventh day, to march seven times. Then, they were to blast the trumpets and shout loudly. Anything less would have been disobedience, and they would have forfeited the fight.

The marching had nothing to do with military tactics and everything to do with a nation learning to walk in step with their God. There would be much bigger fights ahead, and their faithfulness here would teach them how to follow God when they were afraid, when it didn't make sense, and when they had to wait on the promise longer than they thought.

This point must be made clearly if you want to reach the promised land. You can't shortchange the process. You must march seven times. You can't stop on three, and you better not stop on six. If Israel would have stopped before the seventh march on the seventh day, it would have been like our family taking up residence at the Worm Motel and sending postcards from our new home in the Mojave Desert. Needles wasn't the destination. Pasadena was. Anything less was disobedience and plain foolish.

Often times, God isn't interested in a well-planned strategy. God just wants to know if we trust Him. God wants to know if we'll persevere under the pressure. God is doing something in us; He's fortifying us from the inside, and this process cannot be done any other way.

The Apostle Paul is another great teacher in the study of perseverance. He faced many trials and challenges, and his perseverance not only expanded the Kingdom of God, but it also brought growth within him too. "More than that," Paul proclaimed, "we rejoice in our sufferings, knowing that suffering produces endurance, and endurance produces character, and character produces hope, and hope does not put us to shame, because God's love has been poured into our hearts through the Holy Spirit who has been given to us" (Romans 5:3-5 RSV). Paul knew that God reserves great spiritual treasures for those who keep marching, keep driving, and do not give up.

In the crucible, God not only reveals more of Himself. He reveals more of us. It's in the marching, in the driving, in the not giving up that you discover what you're made of. You have more in you than you realize. Within you, there's depth of character that will bring about greater blessing and impact. Within you, there's a hope that will sustain you when the hurts of this broken world intensify. There's a love that will overflow from within—ferociously and steadfastly.

BREAKTHROUGH

Joshua's army marched around the city seven times for the seventh day in a row. During the seventh time, the priests sounded the trumpets, and Joshua commanded the army to shout. The city wall fell, and the army took the city. The people of Israel began to inherit the promised land.

Some people never get to see the promise because they stop on six, or they take up residence in Needles. God's goal for your life is not to have safety and security. God desires for you to live fully, to impact the world with the power of His love, and to experience greater depths of living inside of His love. This is your destiny. And the truth is, to reach this summit, sometimes you'll have to drive through Needles. Sometimes you'll have to march around Jericho and fight some battles. Sometimes you'll have to march when it doesn't make sense. And for those who don't give up, they'll get to see what others only hear about. Their obedience and perseverance will result in new victories, new breakthroughs, and new levels of character and strength.

The Apostle Paul knew hardships that most modern Christians will never experience. This means that Paul experienced greater joy on the other side of the pain than we can scarcely imagine. This is why Paul can boldly instruct us, "And let us not grow weary of doing good, for in due season we will reap, if we do not give up" (Galatians 6:9). I want this for me, and I want it for you. Some days are just tough, and some seasons feel like they'll never pass. I know; I've been there. And while I don't know what you may be facing, I can boldly speak from experience that on the other side of perseverance, there is a great harvest waiting for you.

Don't stop on six. March seven times. Keep on driving. Needles isn't your destination.

QUESTIONS *for* TRANSFORMATION

1. As you look back on your past, what can you learn from times when you quit too soon on the goal?

2. Moreover, how have seasons of perseverance helped you see more of God and what He can do in your life?

3. If you're in a difficult season right now, how can the lesson of Jericho encourage you to remain faithful?

4. Has God been clear with you about an area of your life? Do you feel tempted to stop short? How can Paul's encouragement not to give up fortify you to keep moving ahead?

"Take the first step in faith. You don't have to see the whole staircase, just take the first step."

—DR. MARTIN LUTHER KING, JR.[9]

CHAPTER 5

GO AND I WILL BLESS YOU

In the middle of downtown Pasadena sits the beautiful campus of Fuller Theological Seminary. Fuller is comprised of historic craftsman homes converted to office buildings, a modern all-glass library with an open-air roof, and massive palm trees everywhere, all set against the majestic backdrop of the Sierra Madre mountains.

My favorite spot on the campus was perhaps its most overlooked feature: a prayer garden tucked away on the south end of campus. It was set aside as an urban oasis from the busyness that surrounded. In my experience, this is where real work is done. And as our time in Los Angeles was waning, my time in the prayer garden increased. I had moved my family across the country with a plan. Along the way we also expanded, adding a second daughter, sweet Ella, to our family. Now, after two years of living in Southern California, we had mostly drained our savings, and we weren't sure what to do next.

DETOURS

My ultimate goal was to become a professor of theology and culture at a top-tier university. However, there were detours and roadblocks along this path. To apply for post-graduate programs in America, most institutions have desired scores for their applicant base. In my case, applying for doctoral programs at a top-tier school required scores in the top one percent.

My scores on the Graduate Record Examination weren't at the level I needed. I would either have to spend lots of time and money (we had neither) studying at a testing center in hopes of raising my score a few percentiles, or we'd have to find another path. I applied for and was accepted into PhD opportunities at four schools in the United Kingdom (this was possible because they don't utilize standardized testing). I was also accepted into an advanced master's program at Duke University. Duke was my top choice, and there was a professor who wanted me to study with him.

All of these options required lots of money and a big transition for our family. None of them offered max scholarships, and none of them had job opportunities waiting for us. We considered abandoning the plan altogether.

ALL THINGS WORK TOGETHER FOR GOOD

Throughout our journey, there have been times when we've discerned God's voice clearly directing our steps, moving us down a particular path to a specific destination. At other times, there has been a passion burning from within beckoning us forward. However, there have also been seasons when we have been confused and scared, feeling like we had completely missed an important turn along the way.

The good news is that God is good, all-powerful, and redemptive. So, even if we blow it (and we *will* mess up), God can get us to our purpose. Again, the psalmist proclaims, "The Lord will fulfill his purpose for me; your steadfast love, O Lord, endures forever" (Psalm 138:8).

Rather than worrying if we have "found God's will" or if we have wandered outside it, we can focus on pursuing God in relationship while takings steps of faith in full view of God's steadfast love and power. The Apostle Paul would regularly make plans and at the same time move with God's Spirit. It's why he could boldly believe, "And we know that for those who love God all things work together for good, for those who are called according to his purpose" (Romans 8:28).

WHAT TO DO WHEN YOU DON'T KNOW WHAT TO DO

Wouldn't it be great if everything fell into place when you chose to live fully? It would be awesome if next steps were always clear and the resources needed to take them were readily available.

But what do you do when you don't know what to do? This is an important question, and it's likely that you'll ask it many times over the course of your life. There isn't an easy, one-size-fits-all answer because God wants to develop you beyond your current capacities. But while the answers won't be easy, there are some heart postures that can guide you to making God-honoring decisions.

I prayed like never before. I made the prayer garden my second home. I declared along with the prophet Samuel, "Thus far the Lord has helped us" (1 Samuel 7:12 NIV). God had brought us too far to abandon us. Even if we couldn't see it, we were confident that God would fulfill He purpose in our lives.

As I sat in the prayer garden day after day, I discerned a common response from God: "Go and I will bless you."

I need You to tell me what to do, I kept responding.

But that wasn't God's plan for us in this step of our journey. God said, "Go and I will bless you."

I know it can seem counterintuitive, but honestly, it's better this way. If next steps were no-brainers and resources were always plentiful, you wouldn't have to think, and action wouldn't require faith. God's goal for your life is not ease and safety. God wants you to think critically, to determine passionately, and to trust unreservedly. This kind of living is forged in the fire, and if you take the prior chapter to heart, you'll come out better on the other side.

It reminds me of Thomas Merton's prayer of faith even when he could not see his path ahead: "My Lord God, I have no idea where I am going," he confessed. "But I believe that the desire to please you does in fact please you . . . Therefore, I will trust you always, though I may seem to be lost and in the shadow of death. I will not fear for you are ever with me, and you will never leave me to face my perils alone."[10]

PUT IN THE WORK

In my ministry residency at Mosaic, we were told that we would never see a platform. In fact, leadership would be earned and never given. We would start serving in the most unnoticeable areas and graduate to areas of interest only after we put in the work and invested in people along the way. The leadership principle was simple: Nothing is beneath us, and building teams is essential. I cannot overstate the value of this. Every leader must understand what they ask of others, and they must show that every piece of the puzzle is important. If you can't display this, people may follow you, but not for long.

Mosaic has long been an innovator in the church world. They were among the first to reimagine where a church could meet, and how to transform secular spaces into sacred environments. Mosaic also met at the Mayan, originally a theater dedicated to Mayan gods, and was at the time a nightclub and concert venue. Bands like Coldplay had famously gotten their first gigs in L.A. at the Mayan, and every weekend, it was a central L.A. destination. But on Sundays, it was church.

Imagine transforming a space that has wooden gods fashioned on the walls and ceilings, lights on the floor, and a full bar on the stage. As awesome as it was to transform this club into a life-giving church on Sunday evenings, let's not glamorize the process. Sunday afternoon, a team would have to clean and disinfect two stories of mayhem from the night before. We carefully removed needles from urinals and mopped vomit from the floors. We vacuumed carpets, wiped sticky counters, and covered the full bar in drapes. When you're toiling away, wondering if anyone notices, these will be some of your best moments. If no one else notices, God notices.

One of the most important lessons I've learned along the way is this: There are no shortcuts. I'm always looking for smarter and faster ways to do almost everything. But when it comes to living fully and immersing yourself into your God-given destiny, nothing will substitute for hard work. In fact, I'm convinced that if you keep showing up with a great attitude, put in the work, and continue growing, you'll bypass ninety percent of the people around you.

RETAIN OPENNESS TO GOD

As you seek to live out God's purposes for your life, some things will become fixed, but you also need to retain an openness to God. For instance, I know that I'm called to communicate and to lead. If I did not do these things,

I would be disobedient. Until God says otherwise, these are fixed. How I manifest these callings can have some variation. I'm a planner and a strategist, so we went to Los Angeles with a plan. God likes it when we make plans to live our lives most fully. However, if we don't continually offer those plans to God with open hands, they can become an errant idol and prevent us from walking with God's Spirit.

Remaining open to God is about learning to fix some things in our hearts while also maintaining a vibrant relationship with God to determine His desires, preserving our readiness to change along the way.

YES AND AMEN

As our Good Father, God wants to bless you. When your obedience and openness meet His timing, you'll see an abundance of favor well up in your life. It's why the Apostle Paul confidently declares, "For all the promises of God in Him are Yes, and in Him Amen, to the glory of God through us" (1 Corinthians 1:20 NKJV). And while every step wasn't easy or without its challenges, we've certainly experienced the *Yes and Amen* blessings of God.

God had encouraged us to choose our next step. Eventually, we chose to pursue the advanced master's program at Duke University. We were going to move to Durham, North Carolina, sight unseen. If God said that He would bless us, that was enough for us to move forward.

We had reached an agreement to rent a home near Duke's campus. On the day the movers arrived at our apartment in Pasadena (no more cross-country trailer pulls for us), I received a disturbing email. The owner of the home changed his mind and had decided to sell the house. We had lost a house that we had never seen while shipping our belongings to a city we had never visited. Then, only minutes later, a church in Durham called us and said they were interested in hiring me. The next day, our family flew back to Indiana to visit with family for a few weeks while the few personal possessions we had made their way from the Pacific Coast to the Atlantic Coast. Within days, I hopped on a plane to visit Durham, to interview for a job, and to find us a home, all expenses paid.

We had no idea that we'd eventually connect with a church in Durham that would springboard us headfirst into the favor of God. Just minutes from the home we eventually found, Newhope Church invited me to join their staff as a teaching pastor. In time, my leadership opportunities grew and expanded, and I partnered with a world-class staff. We had a front-row seat to a church that was rapidly growing and seeing many lives transformed. At this time, Newhope was one of the top five fastest growing churches in America. If this weren't enough, we found lifelong friends to journey alongside.

While Duke had been the driver for the destination, education had actually moved to the background for me. I successfully completed my studies at Duke, and we decided to hit the pause button on a PhD. Our girls were young and growing fast, and we were now welcoming our son to the family. As you might imagine, studying at Duke was intense and required long hours of study. Add to this the dedication needed to work at a fast-growing church, and there was little time to be a dad. Soon after we decided not to pursue my PhD for the foreseeable future, I sat next to a tenured professor at a speakers' dinner for a conference. We struck up a friendship and within months, I was invited to become an adjunct professor at Indiana Wesleyan University, where I've served for several years. Moreover, that open door has also led to the opportunity to serve as adjunct professor of bible, theology, and church history at Southeastern University.

When Katie and I would reflect on the adventurous drive from rural Indiana to Southern California, only to be experiencing God's favor in North Carolina, we can only contemplate the psalmist's words, "Surely your goodness and unfailing love will pursue me all the days of my life . . ." (Psalm 23:6 NLT). You are made to live! God desires to expand your life and to flood your life with blessings. God wants to use the blessings in your life to flood His Creation with His love. When you choose to live for God and in God, watch out. In Jesus, all the promises of God are *Yes and Amen*!

QUESTIONS *for* TRANSFORMATION

1. Most people lean toward advance planning or spontaneity. Which side do you naturally gravitate to?

2. What will you do when you don't know what to do? What foundational elements will guide you on the journey?

3. Do you believe that God longs to bless you as you faithfully pursue Him and His mission? Why do you find this easy or hard?

4. What does it mean for you to be fixed on a plan while also allowing for God's movement in your life?

*"We shall not cease from exploration
And the end of all our exploring
Will be to arrive where we started
And know the place for the first time."*

—T.S. ELIOT[11]

CHAPTER 6

DON'T WASTE
THE WAITING

I'm not the world's biggest fan of winter.

I love living in a place where you can experience all four seasons. I just wish the cold one lasted for about a month and then moved on. Growing up in the Midwest, it never occurred to me that winter was optional. And then we moved to Southern California, where fall and winter each last about two weeks with an additional week of rain. When we moved to North Carolina, however, I experienced my first legitimate spring season.

What transpires in the Carolinas from February through May is spectacular. I had never seen so many colors, so many sunny days with temperatures in the sixties and seventies with a perfect light breeze. On days like those, it should be legally required to open all windows in the house. What I thought was a throwaway season became my favorite.

One year, North Carolina had a particularly harsh and long winter. Springtime reminded me more of the Midwest than a southern coastal state. If it wasn't snowing, it was raining, and it was far too cold to open any windows. But one Sunday, the spring season broke through in remarkable fashion. The sun was beaming in a cloudless sky, birds were singing, and the warmth had finally come.

We lived in a neighborhood near the church where I served, and with a long walk, I could get there on foot. Since it was so beautiful, I left early so that I could fully appreciate and enjoy the new season. As I walked along with the warmth on my skin, I began to worship God. I was thanking God for every color that was blossoming, for the sun that was shining, and for having good health to walk. If it came to my mind, I was thanking and praising God with vigor.

As I began to pat myself on the back for such extraordinary adoration, God decided to break through the noise. Sometimes God speaks to me in a gentle whisper, reminding me that He is close and caring, affirming His unending love for me. This was not one of those moments.

"Chad," He said, "I wish you would thank Me in every season."

Mic dropped. Enough said. God out.

I went from basking in the sunshine to wishing I could find a place to hide. At first, I thought, "Wow, this is the thanks I get for my remarkable praise and worship?" But as the Holy Spirit continued to speak to my spirit, I knew this was conviction I desperately needed. Of course I had been praising God for the spring season (and wishing away the lingering winter), but God wasn't really talking about the weather, and I knew it. God was talking about the seasons of life. Far too often, I had wished away challenging seasons in my life and my family's life rather than engaging with and learning from them. As the long winter months dragged on, we were also walking through a challenging season in our lives, and I wanted it to be over.

As we run after God's purpose for our lives, there will be seasons. Some will feel like everything is blossoming and growing, and in others, it will feel like the intense heat of summer. Sometimes life will feel as pleasant as your most comfortable sweatshirt with hot apple cider in your favorite mug, watching the orange and red leaves fall as you stroll amidst a row of changing trees. But some seasons will wear on your soul like a long winter, heavy with snow and bone-chillingly cold.

But remember this: God makes every season. There are some things that God can teach you only in these seasons, and if you miss it, you miss it. Or, if God really wants you to learn the lesson, you'll have to engage the season again.

Remember, God's goal for you is not to arrive safely at a destination but to develop your character and to grow your capacity for experiencing and sharing His love. God can't expand your life without stretching your soul. To maximize every season God walks you through, you must live thankful in every season. If your heart is open to God, all the seasons matter, and they all have divine purpose. The question is, are you engaging them purposefully?

THE GLOOM OF HOLY SATURDAY

In the Church, everyone loves to celebrate Easter Sunday! Not only is the sun beginning to shine outside, but it's when we rejoice over the Son rising up from the dead. Jesus triumphed over death and the grave, making a way to new life for every person who calls on His name.

We even glory in the cross, labeling that day "Good Friday." While we mourn the reality that God's Son was brutally murdered, we exult because the perfect Lamb of God paid the penalty for our sins. The innocent died for the guilty. Jesus took our brokenness and gave us His righteousness. Good Friday and Easter Sunday are great cause for remembrance.

However, most Christians today are unaware of Holy Saturday. On this day, the followers of Jesus were overcome with grief, confusion, and fear. They had left everything to follow Jesus. Now, they were hiding behind locked doors, uncertain of their fate. With the privilege of hindsight, we know all about Easter Sunday. We know that Jesus would turn the world upside-down and that the disciples would carry His name all over the Mediterranean. But in their timeline, in their lives, Sunday hadn't come, and the One they pursued, the One they boldly followed and proclaimed all over the Jewish world, was just brutally murdered.

For us, the cross represents how Jesus separated us from our sin and the empty tomb signifies the promise of new life. But we also must remember the importance of Holy Saturday and it's this: sometimes we wait. Often grief, anguish, sorrow, and unknowns linger longer than we want. These are winter seasons of the soul, and while they frequently subside more slowly than we'd like, they have a purpose.

Winter allows the earth to rest from its toil and prepare for both the growth and the harvest to come. Without winter, there is no growth. Without growth, there is no harvest. They all have a role to play. And the message to us from God is clear: Don't waste the waiting. As we wait, God is fortifying and strengthening our souls. God is developing our character. God is cultivating in us what He'll do through us in the coming seasons. But if you waste the waiting with a bitter heart or an escapist mindset, you'll forfeit the wisdom that God aspires to produce in you, and—in time— what God wants to bring out of you into the world.

ACT LIKE YOU'VE BEEN HERE BEFORE

I'm a huge sports fan! I cannot tell you the number of times I've heard an old curmudgeon of a coach or an announcer repeat the words, "Act like you've been here before." This is usually in reference to an overzealous player wildly celebrating a triumphant play over an opponent. I become a curmudgeon whenever a player celebrates a small success during the game but the team is losing. I like to win, and celebrating your own success while the team is behind feels like a participation trophy.

This phrase should also echo in our souls when we traverse a difficult season. As a follower of Jesus, He told us that in life we would have troubles (John 16:33). But Jesus also told us to take heart because He has already overcome them. Yet when we encounter a challenging time of life, we typically act like our world is coming to an end. Bitterness sets in. Confusion swirls in our minds. We forget how God has faithfully led us through trying times before. Actively seeking to avoid a tough season is a grave mistake because God wants to redeem the challenges to grow our dependency on Him. If we forget His faithfulness, we miss the point entirely.

In the Old Testament, God knew that Israel had a memory problem. For instance, after He mightily led them out of Egypt, they were afraid to enter the promised land. Consequently, they wandered for forty years, and a whole generation died without inheriting their God-given promise. So, after they miraculously cross the River Jordan to finally enter the promised land, they stack twelve stones so that future generations remember God's faithfulness (Joshua 4).

"When you stood on the brink of the promise," God was retelling them, "your feet walked into the flood waters of the Jordan and I led you across on dry ground, just as I had done before." But God wasn't just reminding future generations. He was also marking the minds of the current generation. God was championing them, "With every battle you're about to fight, remember that I am mighty and that I am with you."

When God sees you through a hard time in life, you need to find a way to mark it. The Israelites set up stones. You may need to write your testimony in a journal, snap a photo, take a trip, or share it with someone else. We are victims of the moment, and our memories need help. Perhaps one of the saddest passages in the Bible comes just one book later: "After that whole generation had been gathered to their ancestors, another generation grew up who knew neither the LORD nor what he had done for Israel" (Judges 2:8-10 NIV).

If you're in a challenging time in your life right now, don't waste the waiting. Lean into God. Look back on His faithfulness in your past. If you're on the mountaintop today, this is the time to mark prior victories so that you cling to God's faithfulness in the next valley. Don't forget to remember.

PASS THE TEST BEFORE YOU LEVEL UP

I've often had the opportunity of coaching sports teams that my kids play on. Honestly, it's one of the great privileges of my life. Recently while coaching my son's baseball team, we were using a throwing machine to give the boys an opportunity to shag grounders and fly balls. When we switched to pop-ups, only about a third of them were catching the balls. Yet, all the boys kept asking me to turn the machine on high. They wanted to watch how high the baseballs could go in the air. But all I cared about was helping them learn to catch. I kept stopping to teach them how to get under the fly balls and they kept chanting "turn it up!" Finally, I shouted back, "If you'll catch the ball on the low setting, then I can turn it up." In other words, if you'll show ability at one level, I can take you to a new level.

A similar thing happens with my kids quite often. They'll ask about the permission to do something like going for a long walk in our neighborhood, or staying home by themselves, or getting a smartphone, and in time, it will be to drive a car and so forth. When Katie and I ask them to do something simple like, pick up your clothes, be kind to each other, help clean the house, and so on, we're watching for faithfulness. We'll tell them, "You're asking to do things that require trust. We're asking you to do what you're told. If you can do what you're told, we can trust you with greater responsibility." Just like I was asking the boys to pay attention and catch the fly balls, we're asking the kids to earn greater levels of trust.

God works like this too. "God, do great things in and through my life," we'll pray. "God, please bless my income and give me more ministry," we'll continue. But I often think God is responding, "Do the last thing I told you, and then I can give you more." We have yet to pass the elementary test, but we're asking for graduate-level responsibilities. Sometimes we just need to do what we're told.

When considering greater levels of trust and opportunity, we need to look no further than the Israelites in this period between the Exodus and the entry to the promised land. They wanted to be anywhere but roaming aimlessly in the desert, but they didn't do what they were told. God told them to inherit their promise, but instead, they chose to disobey. They allowed fear to dictate their destiny. An entire generation left Egypt, they witnessed God part the Red Sea, but all of them died without seeing the promise—everyone except Joshua and Caleb.

When the ten spies came back proclaiming that the land was good but that the people were too strong, they declared that God was true to His word but incapable of leading them to victory. Therefore, they forfeited their inheritance. Even when in the minority, Joshua and Caleb remained steadfast: "Let us go up at once and occupy it, for we are well able to overcome it" (Numbers 13:30). Caleb was forty years old at the time, and he was resolute in believing God for the ability to bring the victory.

What I love more than Caleb's forty-year-old response is his eighty-five-year-old response. Even after wandering in the desert for forty years, and then after helping the other tribes of Israel inherit their promise, Caleb was still ready to fight for his own inheritance.

"And now, behold, the LORD has kept me alive, just as he said, these forty-five years since the time that the LORD spoke this word to Moses, while Israel walked in the wilderness. And now, behold, I am this day eighty-five years old. I am still as strong today as I was in the day that Moses sent me; my strength now is as my strength was then, for war and for going and coming. So now give me this hill country of which the LORD spoke on that day." . . . Therefore Hebron became the inheritance of Caleb the son of Jephunneh the Kenizzite to this day, because he wholly followed the LORD, the God of Israel. (Joshua 14:10-14)

At eighty-five, Caleb was still ready to fight! He knew that God was able then and he believed that God was able now. How could he be so certain that God could use an eighty-five-year-old man? Caleb wasn't concerned with his age because he knew it wasn't about his age forty-five years earlier. It was always about the faithfulness and might of his God.

Everyone else lost faith, died, and missed out, but Joshua and Caleb remained full of faith and got to see the promise. This truth is still relevant today. Too many people quit and turn back and never get to see God's strength. They never see the promises that God would love to pour into their lives because they aren't willing to fight through the tough seasons. They aren't willing to simply do what God told them to do. Joshua and Caleb knew they'd have to show up for the fight, but they also knew they'd never fight alone.

God loves to graduate us and move us to greater levels of faith and impact. However, we must first pass the test in front of us. God won't give us more until we prove faithful with what's before us. We must not wait for some day in the future when everything is perfect and all the pieces line up. Right now, we must do what God has told us to do: Live with integrity, get rid of that sinful behavior or attitude, remain faithful in a tough season, give generously, love freely, forgive extravagantly, and honor the leader(s) in your life. I don't know what God is asking you to do, but I'm guessing you have an idea. Do the last thing God told you to do for as long as God asks you to do it. Do what you're told, and watch God show Himself faithful and mighty in your life.

EMBRACE THE SEASON

Considering how many sports seasons I played growing up, it's no small miracle that I played every season to completion. Believe me, there were plenty of times that I wanted to quit, but my parents wouldn't let me. If I started a season, I had to finish it. During my junior year of high school, I broke my wrist during the final week of summer practice for football. Even then, I put on a cast and kept playing. Our team lost every game that season. And to top it off, my cast wasn't removed until the week after our final game. Every time I had to go to the doctor to change my cast because it was full of grass and dried mud, not to mention the smell from teenage sweat, I wanted to quit. My dad's voice rings in my mind today: "Chad, if you quit now, you'll quit important things all your life." I didn't know then just how right he was.

Sometimes the most spiritually healthy thing you can do is to continue to show up and go all-in, especially when you don't feel like it. And don't just show up; embrace the season that God has you in. Here's what I've learned: When you choose to embrace the season you're in, then God will unveil all that this season has to embrace. Once you commit to being fully present, you make it possible for God to open your eyes to all that He wants you to see. When you walk in bitterness and frustration, your hard heart shuts you down spiritually. When you're trying everything in your power to run from the season, your spiritual receptors stop working.

God is faithful and God is moving, even when you can't see it. "Not one of all the LORD's good promises to Israel failed; every one was fulfilled" (Joshua 21:45 NIV). If God is faithful and God will bring His promise about, we should protect our hearts and remain steadfast with God. If we don't, God may choose to bring us into the promise, but we will have missed the opportunity for growth. If we cling tighter to God in the midst of the hardship, not only will God prove faithful, but we will move through the valley with God, and thus we'll emerge with more character, greater wisdom, and fuller faith.

HONOR IS A KEY THAT UNLOCKS MANY DOORS

When it feels like you're waiting on your big break, the best thing you can do is serve the vision of a leader above you. It's called honor, and nothing will promote you faster. The sooner you can learn to honor others, the sooner God can advance you as a leader. Naturally, young leaders want to demonstrate their abilities. And they want seasoned leaders to notice them. But what most young leaders don't know is that honor is a key that unlocks many doors.

When we read the Bible, most of us assume the greats started out that way. We think they didn't have to work for the greatness, it was just born within them. However, it's important for us to realize that they are just like us, and they too must work to live their best story. They must put in the time when it seems like no one is looking. They aren't overnight sensations; they are people that refused to stop growing and serving.

In these waiting seasons, most people ask themselves very similar questions.

"Does anyone notice?"

"What's the point?"

"Do my efforts matter?"

"Do I make a difference?"

The prophet Elisha shows us that the season we inhabit today is the most important season. Who you are today will determine who you become in the future when you finally land the dream job and the ideal situation.

Today matters, and when we think no one sees us, we must remember that God is watching. When you feel insignificant, overlooked, and underappreciated, keep putting in the hard work.

Elisha becomes one of the greatest prophets in the Old Testament, but he began in total obscurity. We should never judge where God can take us based on where we are today. In fact, when the great prophet Elijah selects Elisha as his successor, he finds Elisha in an unenviable place.

> So he departed from there and found Elisha the son of Shaphat, who was plowing with twelve yoke of oxen in front of him, and he was with the twelfth. Elijah passed by him and cast his cloaking upon him. And he left the oxen and ran after Elijah . . . (1 Kings 19:19-20).

Regardless of your vocation, you can do important work wherever God has you. That said, Elisha's job stank. Literally. Not only did he make his living looking at the back side of oxen every day, but he was on the twelfth pair. So, eleven pair of oxen went before him, which meant their monstrous droppings went before as well. And even if he loved his job, I'm guessing there were days when he felt insignificant. Each day, he'd lock in and work behind two stinky behinds. Some of you work with some stinky behinds, and you think, "There's got to be more to this life. Surely, I have more to offer than this."

While we don't know much about Elisha's life before Elijah's call, he was a great farmer. How do I know this? Because God wouldn't have selected him otherwise. I don't know how skilled of a farmer he was, but I know that he worked hard. Elisha learned to give his best wherever God placed him. If there's one thing Elisha knew, it was the law of sowing and reaping. The Apostle Paul said it this way: "If you think you can fool God, you are only fooling yourselves. You will harvest what you plant" (Galatians 6:7 ERV).

Elisha gets the promotion because no one plowed straighter lines, got up earlier, or worked later. He honored his boss by working hard. If he hadn't, God wouldn't have promoted him. He wasn't even found looking for another job—he was just being faithful where God had placed him. Everyone wants the big promotion, but very few people are willing to put in the work to earn it. Doing things God's way always precedes God's will transpiring in our lives. Elisha was faithful day in and day out, and he reminds us that we should give God our best when we think no one is watching. He was appointed to become a prophet and it was not because he was already a great communicator. All we know was that he was a faithful farmer. In time, he would do twice as many miracles as did his mentor Elijah, but that's not where he started.

WAITING WITH EXCELLENCE

When it seems like no one is paying attention, God is watching closely. It's why Jesus told His followers, "Then your Father, who sees what is done in secret, will reward you" (Matthew 6:4 NIV).

Even when we're unsure if the work is important, we must keep giving our very best. Again, Jesus encourages us, "'Whoever can be trusted with very little can also be trusted with much, and whoever is dishonest with very little will also be dishonest with much'" (Luke 16:10 NIV). Jesus wants us to know that not only is God watching, but God is setting up our next assignments based on what we do with our current opportunities. Your heart and your work *now* determine what you get to do next. There are no shortcuts to impact. God cannot graduate you to what's next until you're faithful right where you are.

In my leadership journey, there were times when I felt like no one noticed me. No one cared if I served and no one saw what I did. This was especially true when I served as a ministry resident amidst a large multisite church in L.A. But there was one guy that would always propel me forward. His name was Miguel, and he was always around. When I showed up early in Pasadena, Miguel would help me set up the tents. When I showed up on Sunday afternoons to help transition the nightclub into a church, Miguel would have a vacuum, already cleaning the floors. When I'd leave to go home and see my family, Miguel would be in the parking lot. What I came to learn is that all the ministry residents serving at the other campuses also knew Miguel. After he was done in Pasadena, he'd go to Beverly Hills and help them. Then, he'd drive to Santa Monica and help them before ending his day at the nightclub downtown.

Once a year, we'd gather all the campuses together for a day of vision and celebration. The pinnacle moment each year was when we'd recognize the volunteer leader of the year. Servanthood was a core value, so we'd recognize the person that best modeled it for the rest of us. This particular year, as the day grew into evening, everyone anticipated the opportunity to celebrate the volunteer leader of the year. Leadership spoke on the value and purpose of the award. Then, they began to recount how this year's winner so faithfully served. And then, as they voiced Miguel's name, the whole place erupted. The only person who was surprised? Miguel. He walked on stage—this middle-aged tough guy, weeping like a baby. He just kept saying, "I didn't think anyone noticed."

And then I remember our pastor saying, "Miguel, look at the crowd. Do you see how they're cheering? Miguel, we all noticed!"

When he served, he gave his best even when he thought no one was looking. He gave his best when it seemed insignificant. He gave his best because God was his audience. With his heart posture, Miguel gave me a master's degree in servant leadership.

GOD-CONFIDENT

When Elisha followed Elijah, he had no idea what was ahead. But that didn't stop him from following. Elisha reminds us that we can fully place our trust in God even when we don't wholly understand what's ahead. Elisha didn't ask about the compensation and benefits package. He didn't check to see if it came with good health insurance. He just went. To be sure, these are both great things, and perhaps they're important to you in your next step. My bigger point is that we can trust God with these kinds of details.

> "So don't worry about these things, saying, 'What will we eat? What will we drink? What will we wear?' These things dominate the thoughts of unbelievers, but your heavenly Father already knows all your needs. Seek the Kingdom of God above all else, and live righteously, and he will give you everything you need. So don't worry about tomorrow, for tomorrow will bring its own worries. Today's trouble is enough for today." (Matthew 6:31-34 NLT)

You don't have to know the whole path; you just need to take your next step. I know it can be scary trying something new. But remember, you can fully trust God without wholly understanding the journey. What next step is God inviting you to take?

DON'T WASTE THE WAITING

For ten years, Elisha did seemingly trivial work. For example, one of his jobs was to wash Elijah's hands. It might have been cool for a couple of weeks, maybe even a couple of months. *It's Elijah, the great prophet, and I get to serve him*, he may have concluded. But eventually, he may have thought, *Wash your own hands, Elijah. You're a grown man. I'll show you where to find the towel and water, but I'm ready to lead.* But for ten years, what God had said did not yet match what Elisha saw in front of him. And one of the things I love about Elisha's honor to Elijah and faithfulness to God is that we can serve diligently even when what you see doesn't yet match what God said.

Maybe you're in a waiting season today. Perhaps it kind of feels like someone has hit the "pause" button on your life. But remember this: When you serve God wholeheartedly, even when it seems like nothing is progressing, much is still accelerating in the spiritual realm. When you honor the leaders above you and faithfully serve the opportunities before you, God is watching, and God is advancing His Kingdom through your life.

Maybe you're waiting on your marriage to turn around. Perhaps you're hoping for children of your own. Maybe you're hoping to get married. Perhaps you're praying for your children to follow Jesus. Or you're wondering when this health problem will pass. I want to implore you today to have faith, even when what you see has yet to match what God has said. God is for you. God loves you. God made you, and God will bring His purpose to the forefront in your life. If you've been wondering if what you do matters, if anyone notices, or if there's more purpose coming your way, keep being faithful. Keep honoring the leaders and the people God has in your life right now. Serve God unreservedly right where you are. Honor and faithfulness are powerful values that greatly accelerate God's purpose in your life. Don't waste the waiting.

QUESTIONS *for* TRANSFORMATION

1. As you look back on your life, can you identify times when you wasted the waiting season?

2. Going forward, how can you remind yourself and others of God's faithfulness and the importance of the waiting seasons?

3. How will you learn from God in the waiting season rather than run from God?

4. Is there a leader that you need to honor in this season of your life? Is there a leader from a prior season that you need to appreciate?

5. How can you be most faithful to God right where you are?

ATTRIBUTE 3
MADE *to* SERVE

Defeat Distraction, Smash Selfishness, Axe Apathy

"'Let your light so shine everywhere you go . . . so men and women everywhere may see your good actions, may see creation at its fullest, may see your devotion to Me, and may turn and praise your Father in heaven because of it.'"
—Matthew 5:16 VOICE

"Simple can be harder than complex. You have to work hard to get your thinking clean to make it simple. But it's worth it in the end because once you get there, you can move mountains."

—STEVE JOBS[12]

CHAPTER 7

PICK A FIGHT
WORTHY OF YOUR LIFE

By all accounts, it was a beautiful Friday. In fact, it was Good Friday. So, when I heard the scream, I was horrified. I'll never forget the sound, and I hope that I'll never hear it again.

I had spent the morning serving communion to members of our church family. Just seven months prior, God had provided a tremendous opportunity for us. I was now serving as the pastor to Pinelake Church's Reservoir Campus just east of Jackson, Mississippi. We purchased a home in the suburban community of Brandon. We had an amazing backyard complete with a pool, firepit, and an outdoor living space. We loved everything about it except for one thing: the wildlife. For two people who grew up in Indiana, Mississippi wildlife was a new adventure. Our home was backed against a wild nature area, so almost daily we met new *neighbors*, including unidentifiable lizards, armadillos, wolf spiders as big as your hand, and snakes . . . lots of different kinds of snakes.

Now afternoon, the kids had just finished swimming in the pool and I had just sat down after several hours of yardwork. I decided to watch TV in our outdoor living area while Katie was doing some light work on our many rose bushes in the backyard. And that's when it happened. The pitch and volume of the scream was somewhere between the terror of someone being abducted and the pain of someone being brutally attacked. It was awful. I jumped out of my seat and turned to see Katie running in our backyard. I ran to her, trying to learn what was happening while also looking for a possible murderer inside of our fence. Between sobs and hyperventilating, Katie was able to stammer the word, "S-s-s-snake! I was bitten by a s-s-snake!"

By this time, our children had emerged from the house and saw Katie in pain and shock. She ran to them and asked them to stay inside while pointing me in the direction of the snake. At the time, I didn't know much about the difference between venomous snakes and harmless snakes. The Midwest doesn't prepare you for Southern living. However, I had pulled several snakes from the pool skimmer, a dreadful routine and ritual I'd repeat during the years we lived there. In my mind, all snakes were bad, and I assumed that all of them desired to destroy me. Thus, any snake entering our property was met with the same fate: sudden death.

I began looking for this snake in the area where Katie was pointing. Pine straw surrounded the perimeter of our pool and was spread all the way to our fence. While beautiful, it was easy for snakes to blend in. Unable to see what I presumed was an Amazonian Python, I bent over, looking closely, and discovered a multi-colored snake coiled up and camouflaged in the straw. At this point, my mission was clear: This snake must meet his demise. A swift but agonizing death. I don't know if those two things can go together, but the time for rational thinking had passed. This snake, I presumed, was the very one that had deceived Adam and Eve in the Garden, and it was time for retribution.

Fixing my gaze on the enemy, I asked my snake-bitten bride to fetch me a shovel. Soon she returned and hobbled over with the weapon. I ran to the enemy, raised the blade, and chopped the mighty serpent in two. Justice had been served. That snake was no longer with us. Our yard was restored to peace. My bride was avenged. Though, we still had to get her to the hospital, but more on that later.

If it's not already obvious, I'm not a big fan of snakes. I prefer to avoid them, but if they are within range of my family, they've got to go. I removed and exterminated dozens of snakes from our pool, and I even executed one that decided to enter our home. Our pinewood floor was never quite the same, but things happen in the fog of war. What's my point? When I heard Katie's scream and I saw that snake in my backyard, the reason for my existence was crystal clear: This snake must die. I had to remove it from this world so that my beautiful bride could enjoy our yard again. It had to die because I couldn't stand the thought of it hurting one of our children next.

In much the same way, you need to know the reason for your existence. There are a lot of things you *can* do in life, but what things *must* you do? Here's the way I like to say it: What is a fight worthy of your life?

It will likely take some time to arrive at clarity. In truth, your focus will likely evolve throughout your life. But you must do the hard work of discovering what is worth your time. You get one life on this earth; how will you spend it? None of us know the length of our days.

How will we seize them? What *must* you do? What wrong must you right? What people must you help? How has God uniquely fashioned you? How can your passions align with your compassion? How can your hurts and experiences be redeemed to help others experience hope?

WHAT *MUST* YOU DO?

When the Spirit of God stirs within the spirit of a follower of Jesus, a *must*-ness emerges. Deep within, there is something that they *must* do, something *must* change, something *must* happen, or something *must* be brought into the world. They cannot sit around and do nothing. Innovation *must* be born, justice *must* be served, the hurting *must* be helped.

The words of Joshua Chamberlain come close to articulating this inner desire toward forward movement. Upon receiving the Medal of Honor from President Grover Cleveland, Chamberlain recounts, "I had deep within me the inability to do nothing." Accomplished at many levels, he served as both the Governor of Maine and the president of Bowdoin College. Particularly, though, Chamberlain was referencing his act of courage that possibly shifted the momentum of the Civil War.

On the battlefield in Gettysburg, Pennsylvania, Chamberlain's "inability to do nothing" was on full display. Then the colonel of the Twentieth Maine Volunteer Infantry Regiment for the Union Army, his three hundred soldiers faced the much larger regiments of the Fifteenth and Forty-Seventh Alabama infantry regiments of the Confederate army. On July 2, 1863, at two-thirty p.m., repeated Confederate charges left the Maine regiment with only eighty men. Knocked down by a bullet that hit his belt buckle, Chamberlain stood back to his feet and assessed the dire situation. No reinforcements were coming. The men had only one round of ammunition remaining, and the Alabama regiments were preparing for another assault. His options were to surrender or to attempt forward movement.

"I knew I may die," Chamberlain recalled, "but I also knew that I would not die with a bullet in my back." He had the inability to do nothing, a *must*-ness for his men and his country. Chamberlain scaled their stone barricade, raised his sword, and yelled, "Charge!" The Maine Volunteers fixed bayonets and began running at the Alabama regiments. Catching them off-guard, eighty Union soldiers captured four thousand Confederates in only five minutes.

Chamberlain's *must*-ness initiated one of the most unlikely victories in military history. Soon, the rebels would have won the high ground and if they did, historians believe they would have won the Battle of Gettysburg. If they had won that battle, it's likely they would have won the war. *The inability to do nothing,* this *must*-ness inspired the regiment, turned the battle, and saved the Union.[13]

NOTHING CAN HINDER THE LORD

History is brought about by people with a *must*-ness. Chamberlain could neither retreat nor surrender. He *had to* advance forward or die trying. At that point, it wasn't about his life; it was about the cause bigger than his life. When you're willing to risk it all, you know that you've found your *must*.

King Saul's son, Jonathan, had a *must*-ness. His *must* was the good name of the Lord his God and the flourishing of his people. Even in the face of dreadful probabilities, his faith did not waver. His God was strong and good, and His God was for the people of Israel. Much like his friend David, Jonathan couldn't let the name of the Lord be dragged through the mud.

King Saul had only been on the job for two years, but already he was dropping the ball. Saul retained two thousand men for himself and to Jonathan he allotted one thousand troops. With his smaller force, Jonathan took out a Philistine garrison. Not to be outdone, the Philistines assembled thirty thousand chariots with an additional six thousand horsemen and troops. The odds were three to thirty-six, and Saul made it worse by not following God's commands. Fearful of what would happen, he sought the favor of God in the wrong way. Rather than waiting on the priest Samuel (Numbers 18:7), he offered the priestly sacrifice on his own. The favor of God lifted from Saul, and the slow march toward David as the eventual king of Israel began.

In the wake of these events, Saul and Jonathan's forces scattered in all directions. Some retreated to the hill country, safe from harm's way. Others became traitors and joined the Philistine outposts. Their forces shrank to six hundred. Could it get any worse? Yes, it can! Only Saul and Jonathan had weapons. Evidently, the Philistines had monopolized the production of iron needed for weaponry. Thus, not only did the Philistines have sixty times the manpower, but they also had the only weapons available on the battlefield, save the king and his son.

This is when Jonathan's *must* moment emerged. (Picture Popeye's infamous words, "That's all I can stands. I can't stands it no more!") Jonathan would not sit around while his father allowed the name of the Lord to be tarnished and his people to be defeated. Motioning to his armor bearer, Jonathan said, "'Come, let's go over to the outpost of those uncircumcised men. Perhaps the Lord will act in our behalf. Nothing can hinder the Lord from saving, whether by many or by few'" (1 Samuel 14:6 NIV).

As Jonathan surveyed the challenges, and as he placed them against his God, he could clearly see the outcome: God wins, and it won't even be a fair fight. The size of Saul's forces was of no consequence. Of equally less importance was the dominance of the Philistine army. If God was fighting the battle, nothing could hinder Him from winning, whether few stepped up to fight or many.

But Jonathan also knew something incredibly important: someone must show up to the fight. God would not fight Israel's battle if they were all quaking in their boots, hiding in the hill country. Someone with the *inability to do nothing* had to step forward. Someone with a *must*-ness needed to emerge or the battle was already lost.

God works through His children. It has always been this way. God brings about His plan at the pace of faithful men and women. But take note: You aren't merely God's taskmaster; you are His task. You aren't simply a vessel through which God works; you are the work of God. God doesn't use His children to complete His plan. God uses His plan to complete His children. God won't move until someone *must* do something about a problem they see—until someone raises their hand and proclaims, "Here I am. Send me!" (See Isaiah 6:8)

Jonathan reminds us that the battle does not deserve our fear because nothing can hinder the Lord from saving. However, we should be concerned that no one steps forward, that no one raises their hand. You and I cannot do everything, and we aren't big enough for all of the problems around us. But we *must* do something. There are too many people hurting to sit out of all the fights. There are simply far too many people that don't know God's love and don't realize their God-given potential for us to remain passive. The effects of sin are rampant, and God is looking for people willing to knock down the gates of hell to fight for hope and healing. Children are hungry. People are overwhelmed. Racial injustice is prevalent. Political division is separating us. The regiments of evil are preparing for another attack. The enemy is mocking the name of our God. The people of God have fled to the hills, and it appears that the weapons are few. Which fight will you pick that is worthy of your life?

HEART AND SOUL

Among the most lethal of weapons in the arsenal of our enemy is isolation. Far too often, leaders allow the enemy to cut them off from reinforcements. We must realize that not only are we dead in the water without God fighting our battles, but we must also see that when we live in isolation, we are in the crosshairs of the enemy. If our enemy can make us think that we are alone—that no one else has our problems, no one else has our challenges, no one else thinks our thoughts—then he's got us right where he wants us.

When Jonathan said, "Come let's go over," he wasn't having a dialogue with himself. He's not giving himself a pep talk in the mirror, à la Stewart Smalley from the classic *Saturday Night Live* skit. Jonathan was talking to his armor bearer, and I love the servant's response: "'Do all that you have in mind. Go ahead; I am with you heart and soul'" (1 Samuel 14:7 NIV). His response is all the more incredible when you consider the fact that once the fighting began, the armor bearer would cease to bear arms. As soon as they reached the enemy, his job was to hand the sword over to Jonathan. But this reality didn't cause him one moment's pause. "Go ahead," he said. "I am with you heart and soul." If you've got someone like that in your corner, you can charge hell with a water pistol. And the truth is, you must not go alone. God doesn't want you to. God exists in community: Father, Son, and Holy Spirit. God made us in community: Adam and Eve. So too does God send us in community.

As Jonathan and his faithful armor bearer climbed up the cliff to the Philistine outpost, they immediately took out twenty men. Pick your favorite Marvel superhero and you can begin to see what's happening. But this isn't the magic of Hollywood; this is the power of God through His children. And what transpires next can only be described as miraculous. Panic struck the whole army, and the ground shook. Soon, Saul and the remaining troops saw the commotion from afar and joined in hot pursuit. Then, those hiding in the hill country decided it was time to fight. Not to be left on the wrong side, the traitors who had previously switched over to the Philistines flip-flopped faster than a politician in pursuit of reelection, and they too joined the Israelites. "So on that day the Lord saved Israel," all because one man had the inability to do nothing (1 Samuel 14:23). Jonathan instigated the fight, but he didn't go alone.

I'LL MEET YOU AT THE HOSPITAL

Now, those with high relational IQ and deep compassion for others are wondering, "What happened to Katie? Was she okay? Was the snake venomous?" If you felt as though I left you hanging with the snake bite story, you're right! The story isn't over. After I saw to the snake's demise, I began to examine it to determine if it was venomous. We Hoosiers very rarely see venomous snakes, so I snapped a photo and sent it to several longtime Mississippi natives. Each of them responded quickly with some form of, "Dude! That's a venomous snake! Get Katie to the hospital fast!" Then, in proper southern hospitality, each of them offered to help with the kids. And, in proper Midwestern stubbornness, I assured them that I could take care of everything, including getting Katie to the hospital and keeping the kids calm.

Luckily, one of those on the text thread wasn't buying it. Ryan was among those I was responsible for on our staff at Pinelake. He was one of our amazing kids' pastors, and he sent me a personal text outside of the thread and wrote: "Chad, I'm not that far from you. I'll come to your house and watch the kids while you take Katie to the emergency room."

Once again, I assured Ryan that we'd be fine.

He responded, "It's no problem, Chad. I understand that you're in a hurry. I'll meet you on the way, and I'll take the kids back home. That way, you can focus on Katie."

Once more, I insisted that we'd be fine, and that I was probably already too far down the road at that point.

Soon after, we pulled into the Baptist Medical Center in downtown Jackson and Katie was registered. As I sat there huddled up with my family, I had a really lonely moment. I felt a million miles from home. Katie and I were exhausted from the day of working in the yard. We were scared, and it was just us sitting there, unsure of what was to come. I pulled out my phone and noticed a text that was about fifteen minutes old. It was from Ryan, and it came right after I told him we were already headed to the hospital. He had responded, "No problem, I'll meet you guys at the hospital. I want you to be able to take care of Katie. I'll take care of the kids."

It wasn't one minute later when Ryan walked into the Baptist ER. In that moment, I was so viscerally reminded of the power of presence. My loneliness fled, and I was reminded that we had a church family in Mississippi. Soon, Katie and I were taken back to a room where she was examined, tests were run, and they assured us that while she was indeed bitten by a cotton-mouth snake, no venom had been injected into her body.

For many reasons, I'll never forget that Good Friday. Mostly I'll remember that while I killed the snake, Ryan was the hero of the story. Presence matters, and every one of us needs armor bearers who refuse to leave our side. Pick a fight worthy of your life, but don't go alone. Selecting the right armor bearers is as important as the fight you choose. Once the fight commences, you won't have time to wonder if they're still running with you.

QUESTIONS for TRANSFORMATION

1. As you survey your experiences, your passions, and your past hurts, can you see a thread where God can use your life to make a difference?

2. What distractions should you eliminate so that you can focus on what you *must* do?

3. Take some time to write a list of things that you'd consider fights worthy of your life. Talk with trusted, spiritually minded friends, and ask them to pray with you for focus.

4. Who are the armor bearers already around you? How can you encourage them, and in what ways will you invite them to stand by you? If you don't have them, what steps will you take to pray and seek these kinds of friends? And how will you be an armor bearer to them?

"Courage is not the absence of fear; it is the absence of self. . . . Courage allows us to live free from self-preservation and to live generously creative lives. Courage frees us from the fears that would rob us of life itself."

——ERWIN MCMANUS[14]

CHAPTER 8

DIE UPFRONT SO YOU CAN REALLY LIVE

*J*enga is weird. You don't succeed in the game by winning. You advance by *not losing*.

One block at a time is removed from the tower and placed precariously on the top of the tower. As the game proceeds, the tiny tower begins to sway and move as players attempt to find blocks that are not weight-bearing and maintain the balance on top. All the while, players look on with a mixture of feelings spanning from terror to restrained jubilation. Eventually, a player will be forced to pull a block that holds up a large portion of the higher blocks, or they will set it on top of an under-supported and unbalanced portion of the tower. This is when all the blocks come tumbling down to the horror of the losing player and the now-unrestrained euphoria of the non-losing players. Seriously, think about it: No one wins. In the end, all the blocks fall. You just hope that they don't fall on you.

A lot of people live in the mindset that they don't have to be first; they just don't want to be last. They don't need to have the best life; they just don't want to be the one to have all the blocks of life come crumbling down on top of them. They feel really bad if it happens to someone else, but they also hope that it won't be them. Consequently, their lives resemble the game of *Jenga*, trying to arrive safely at death some day in the distant future while simultaneously stacking up the blocks against the people around them.

"We're all trying to get ahead," they reason. "Someone will get short-changed, but it better not be me." Think about the average day. We want the best parking spot. (Well, everyone but my wife. She prefers to park as far away as possible to avoid extra dings and dents in our car. After twenty years of marriage, I've decided it's not worth the fight.) We honk at the car in front of us if they don't hit the accelerator at the exact moment the light turns green. After all, we didn't budget our time wisely, and now we're late to work. If they don't get out of the way, we're really going to be late. Clearly, it's their fault. They're stacking up the blocks against us. Parents argue over who changed the last diaper or whose turn it is to stay up late with the crying baby.

But please hear me: If you want to follow after Jesus, this isn't how you're called to live your life. Jesus said it this way: "'Whoever wants to be my disciple must deny themselves and take up their cross and follow me. For whoever wants to save their life will lose it, but whoever loses their life for me will find it'" (Matthew 16:24-25 NIV). God's economy is upside down. To find your life, you lose it. In losing your life for Jesus, you truly find it.

GIVE THE BLOCKS A SHOVE

Do you want to really make someone scratch their head? The next time you play *Jenga*, instead of stacking up the blocks one move at a time against your opponents, try this: On your first turn, just push the blocks over as hard as you can. You heard right; give *all* the blocks a shove. There will be a really loud boom, and everyone will be confused. Then, look at your opponents and say, "Great job! You win!"

In truth, this will probably make an awkward moment for the people who were prepared to stack up the blocks against you. But imagine if you lived your life this way. Think about each person that you'll encounter throughout your day. So many are waking up ready to do battle with you and the thousands of others they'll crash into along the way. They'll push the kids out the door and be convinced that they are the only driver on the road who knows the appropriate speed, route, and time one should sit at the light. At work, they'll position themselves to look good in front of others—especially those at the top of the corporate ladder. At the school functions, they'll ensure their kid is first and that they are in charge of it all. They'll be exhausted, but then they will encounter you.

You've already made your choice. You've decided upfront to be *for* them and not *against* them. There's a way to describe this kind of living: self-giving courage. As a follower of Jesus, you aren't playing the game. You've chosen to knock the blocks over and lose upfront so that *they* can win. You see a much different prize. You want to cross the threshold of heaven with as many people on each elbow as possible. In the way of Jesus, this is choosing to die upfront so that you can really live. It's losing your life to find it. Following Jesus is living *like* Jesus, who didn't stack up the blocks against His accusers; Jesus went to the cross so that the sinful could receive grace, so that the guilty could go free. Jesus embodied self-giving courage.

Consider how you're currently living your life and how you may be living against the people around you. Over the next week, start thinking about the little decisions you make throughout the day. Are you stacking up the blocks and doing battle against the people around you? Or are you giving the blocks a good shove at the start of the day so that the people you love and want to find hope will find a willing and ready servant when they crash into you?

SAFE RETURN DOUBTFUL

In December of 1914, Sir Ernest Shackleton set sail with a crew of twenty-seven men. At the helm of the British Imperial Trans-Antarctic Expedition, Shackleton's ambition was to accomplish the first crossing of the Antarctic continent, an achievement he believed to be the final great trek of what was called the "Heroic Age of Exploration." Already a renowned polar explorer, Shackleton's fame and legend grew. No one's for sure, but it is widely speculated that most of his crew responded to this recruitment notice. *Time Magazine* wrote, "Men wanted for hazardous journey. Small wages. Bitter cold. Long months of darkness. Constant danger. Safe return doubtful. Honor and recognition in case of success." Whether this advertisement is tale or truth we cannot know, but this we can: when those men set sail, they left comfort and assurance on the shore in order to accomplish a goal bigger than themselves.[15]

When did we start making following Jesus about ourselves and our comfort? Jesus made it clear: "'Whoever wants to be my disciple must deny themselves and take up their cross and follow me'" (Matthew 16:24-25).

Four men in the Gospel of Mark displayed this posture well. Jesus was back in Capernaum and news had spread as to where he was staying. Soon the house was overflowing with people who wanted to hear Him speak. As the commotion was building, some friends got a wild idea. They had a friend who was paralyzed, and they believed that if they could get him to Jesus, perhaps their friend could walk again.

By the time they arrived, the party had pushed through the doorway and around the house. No one could get in and no could get out. No matter! They climbed up on the roof and tore a hole in it. These were not good house guests, but they were too close to Jesus to turn back. They pulled their friend up on the roof and began to lower him on the mat using ropes. They lowered him . . . right in front of Jesus. Can you imagine how they must have felt? Exhausted. Excited. Fearful. Hopeful. Their muscles were scream-ing, their backs aching. Each of their hands were raw and bloody from the ropes and tearing up the roof. Only then did they perhaps wonder if they did the right thing. What if Jesus wouldn't heal their friend? What would the people say? What would the homeowner do? No matter. They got their friend to Jesus, and this could change everything.

NAMES ON THE JERSEYS

As a lifelong Notre Dame football fan, there are many traditions I love. If you show up in South Bend, Indiana, on Game Day, you'll witness the Player Walk, which is when the world-class athletes collectively walk across campus underneath such legendary sights as "Touchdown Jesus" and the Golden Dome on the Basilica. I'll never forget the first time I witnessed the play-ers enter the North Tunnel of the stadium as the band proclaimed, "Here come the Irish!" Upon departing the locker room and descending down the steps toward the field, each player touches the "Play Like a Champion" sign, preparing their hearts for the battle ahead. At Notre Dame, tradition is para-mount. But perhaps one tradition I respect above the others is that no names are written on the jerseys. In an age when everyone wants to be seen and known, especially in Division One college football, Notre Dame retains this important convention. Why? Because when you're part of Notre Dame, the name on the back is less important than the golden helmet you wear. In other words, it's not about the individual; it's about the team.

I think this is one of the elements that I love most about the story of the paralyzed man. The only designation given is "some men." That's it. We don't know the names on the backs of their jerseys; we just know there were four of them. While most people want recognition for their labor, Jesus always taught that the last will be first, and the first will be last. Jesus was so moved by their faith that the paralyzed man gets more than they all bargained for. They wanted him healed. Jesus saw their faith and raised the stakes; Jesus forgave the man of his sins (Mark 2:1-11).

Too often we fall victim to the belief that only the reputable acts are important. We think that high visibility equals high impact. But the truth is this: In the Kingdom of God, it's often the unseen work that blesses God's heart the most. It's why the Apostle Paul compares the church, or the body of Christ, to a human body. "In fact, some parts of the body that seem weakest and least important are actually the most necessary" (1 Corinthians 12:22). Leaders in the body of Christ are lead *servants* and they aren't looking for the credit.

MISSION IMPOSSIBLE

The men who lowered their paralyzed friend seized the moment to help their friend. If they had waited, or if they had played it safe, we'd never know of them, and their friend would have never put weight on his feet again. There were so many opportunities to turn back, to chicken out, to think to themselves, *This has gone too far.* But anything less than what they did would have forfeited the miracle.

Moreover, we know that their faith couldn't have been accomplished alone. It sounds like the paralytic man was not small; think of an NFL linebacker, not a Kentucky Derby jockey. So, it's a good thing that the four of them decided to work together because once they arrived at the house, their task was just beginning. Since they couldn't get inside, they'd used all their strength and intelligence not only to get themselves on top of the home, but to dig through the roof and hoist this large man to the top, lowering him on ropes. By the time he dropped in front of the eyes of Jesus, these men must have been spent. And while it was tough even to do this together, it would have been impossible to do alone. No one, nor just two guys, could have accomplished that.

You'll be tempted to just go it alone sometimes too. Resist that temptation. Bring others into your journey because we aren't made to carry the burdens alone. Each man needed the others to be all-in. Once they picked a corner of the mat, they were all-in. They literally had to pull their weight. All four had to pull together. And because they did, their friend was never the same.

IT'S TIME TO BE DANGEROUS

Have you ever wondered what it would feel like to fly? I have. For as long as I can remember, I've looked to the sky. My love of flying has morphed into a love for travel as I grow older, but early on, it was just the thrill of soaring. I was not alone in this desire. My older brother, Brock, shared this inspiring dream. If the two of us agreed to something as children, that usually meant grand adventures were ahead. I can't remember whose idea it was (probably mine), but without permission, we began dragging old mattresses from our barn and stacking them below our hay loft. We lived out in the country among the farmlands of Clay County, Indiana. Our parents had purchased an old horse farm surrounded by fields and farmlands as far as the eye could see. Since we had recently gotten new mattresses, these old ones needed a new purpose.

Now stacked *safely* below the hay loft, we ascended the ladder inside the horse stall to the loft. The hayloft was a boy's dream, and it was the location of many imaginary (and might I say *legendary*) battles. As we poked our heads out of the loft to look at our landing pads below, it was almost time for take-off. This was it. I'd finally know what it's like to fly. And while I noticed that the loft seemed higher from up above than it had from the ground below, this was not the time to lose heart. I was too close to the thrill of flying to turn back now. As I backed up to prepare my flight, my mom came running out of our old farmhouse with hands raised.

"Boys! What are you thinking?!" she shouted. "Get back inside! You're going to break your necks."

And just like that, the adventure was over before it really began.

Now, to be clear, this was really good parenting. While I didn't get to realize my dream of flying, I have gotten to realize an even greater dream of staying alive. (Thanks, Mom!) That said, for far too long, followers of Jesus have been told to "get back inside" and play it safe. But I don't think that's what it means to follow Jesus at all. Jesus was dangerous. Jesus found a whip and ran out the money changers inside the temple. Jesus verbally sparred with the religious leaders. He went toe to toe with demons. He carried a cross on His back and was brutally murdered, though he could have stopped it all at any moment. Jesus was a beast. And those of us that bear His name are called to live all-out as well. It's time to be dangerous!

The four men who carried Jesus had a "whatever it takes" mindset. No matter the cost to themselves, they were going to get their friend to Jesus. This was the fight they picked, and there was no turning back. Whatever it took, they'd get their friend to the feet of the One who could walk on water. So much of what it means to follow Jesus requires jumping out of the loft and landing in unchartered territory. That's okay—you don't have to have all the answers. You just have to know the One who does. You don't have to know every step of the journey—you just have to know the One who's gone ahead of you and who has your rearguard too.

Then, once you pick your fight, *fight*. It won't be easy. Don't look for the easy way. If you're going to make a difference, there probably isn't an easy option. Look for the route of calling, the route of impact, the route of legacy. Fix yourself to a "whatever it takes" mindset. If it means getting four people together and carrying a man across town, so be it. If it means tearing open a roof and lowering the man through the roof, so be it. Jesus would never be opposed to us using our brains—most Christians today could stand to live with more discernment—but neither is Jesus opposed to bold action. Bold action, daring steps, and a "whatever it takes" mindset enact the favor, the might, and the movement of God.

MOVE THE ALLIGATORS

As the campus pastor for Pinelake Church's Reservoir Campus, one of my great privileges was leading our team of deacons. We had around one hundred people who signed up to do whatever it took to help people experience the love of Jesus. They'd serve communion on a Sunday to more than six thousand people, and they'd visit the sick in hospitals, care for widows, and load trunks full of food to those in need.

On top of this, they'd also show up days and hours early to clear a space at the Ross Barnett Reservoir in Jackson so that hundreds could get baptized. Once a year, we'd do a large outdoor baptism in our nearby lake. So each year, we'd reserve pavilions and a large grassy area, and then we'd baptize right in the lake. The deacons would arrive over the weekend and begin clearing out the area, including debris, rocks, and limbs. They'd show up again while everyone was in church and continue making sure that there was a clear pathway for people to walk and be baptized, marking off a path with flags.

However, rocks and limbs weren't the primary concern; it was the alligators. I'm not kidding. These deacons would disturb the area all weekend long and then again on Sunday to scare away alligators. Then, during the baptism, they'd create a barrier around the people getting baptized so that if by chance one came back, they'd be the first line of defense. These were some men, y'all!

Even beyond this, the deacons were the first to show up in moments of crisis, times of need, and situations that no one could foresee. They'd sit with members in hospital rooms and serve people who were in their toughest seasons. It was my privilege to remind them that when they showed up at the hospital and it looked bleak, their faith would make the difference. When they arrived at a home up in flames, comforting people who had lost everything, their faith would make the difference. When storms have rocked entire neighborhoods, their faith made the difference. When hope seemed lost and words were few, faith made the difference.

"When Jesus saw their faith, he said to the paralyzed man, 'Son, your sins are forgiven'" (Mark 2:5 NIV). While there is a lot of flash and some fun things that happen in this story, this verse sums it up. These men had great faith; it's what drove them to such crazy actions. And because of their faith, Jesus forgave the paralyzed man of his sins. Soon thereafter, Jesus also healed him physically, but beyond temporal healing, Jesus granted this man forever wholeness with God. Why? Because the four men who carried him had dangerous faith. Let that sink in for a moment. The faith of the friends brought spiritual transformation. This means that your faith and subsequent audacious actions can bring about wholeness and healing for others.

You don't have to have all the answers, but cling to what you know to be true of Jesus. There is hope, and there is a God who is present, powerful, and resounding with love. As followers of Jesus, it's our role to retain this faith and to display it whenever possible. Faith makes the difference.

DON'T LOSE HEART

When you think of living with self-giving courage, who do you picture serving? Think about it for a moment. What's the fight worthy of your life? What's your biggest dream? At some point, you'll need to come back and read this chapter, and you'll need to dial in on these three words: Don't lose heart. Living fully and leading others with self-giving courage is not for the faint of heart. Choosing a fight worthy of your life is not the route of least resistance. But I'm so glad that you aren't looking for the easy way out. You will need to retain this resiliency and not lose heart. There will be moments when it feels like you're taking ten steps forward only to take seven steps back. Don't lose heart. You'll convince yourself that the people or person you're serving will never change. Don't lose heart.

I'm reminded of my Uncle Ron. As a Vietnam veteran, he never fully experienced the freedom that he fought for. After returning from the war, his life was rough. Relational challenges and alcoholism became his daily reality. He lived a hard life. And for many, they would have given up on him, and they would be forgiven if they thought he'd never change and give his heart to Jesus. But his daughter Kelly didn't lose heart. Her faith made the difference.

Eventually, decades of hard living took its toll on his body. When asked to officiate his funeral, I knew it was the right way to serve my family, but I wasn't sure if I could overcome emotions to share about his final days. Fighting back tears, I got to share this story.

My uncle's final days were spent in the hospital surrounded by family. On this particular day, Ron seemed agitated, and Kelly asked him, "Dad, are you scared?"

"Heck yes, I'm scared!" (I'm probably cleaning up the language a little.)

Also present, my sister shared this with him: "Uncle Ron, if you have a relationship with Jesus, you don't have to be scared. Do you have this relationship?"

Without taking a breath, my Uncle Ron responded, "Yes!"

Just to make sure that she was clear, my sister continued, "If you believe that Jesus died on the cross to forgive you of your sins and that He rose from the dead to give you life, Uncle Ron, you don't have to be afraid."

Again, with great confidence my uncle replied, "Yes, and Bert's waiting on me."

Ron had a dear friend and fishing buddy named Bert. (If you have an Uncle Ron, he probably has a fishing buddy with the name Bert!) Bert loved Jesus and regularly shared his faith with Ron. Bert had recently passed away, but before he did, he had the opportunity to lead Ron to faith in Jesus.

As I shared this story at my uncle's funeral, I looked out on my extend-ed family with great compassion for their grief and great passion for their hearts. Between tears, I shared with them that they too could have a rela-tionship with Jesus. My uncle didn't like to say "Goodbye"—it seemed too conclusive for him. Instead, he preferred to say, "See you later." So, I shared that if they too had a relationship with Jesus, they wouldn't have to say "Goodbye" to Uncle Ron; instead, they could say, "See you later."

In addition to two of my children, as I write this book, I've had the privilege of baptizing six people present at Uncle Ron's funeral. One was Kelly, who never lost heart with her dad. Another was Kelly's daughter, both of whom I baptized nearly two years to the date after the funeral. Think about all the people who have retained faith and consider how their faith made the difference in the lives of so many. Don't lose heart.

A DIFFERENT KINGDOM

I suppose that you can forgive a mother for wanting great things for her children. But the timing and the occasion for one mother's question to Jesus was, at best, in poor taste—and outright blind ambition at worst. This mother's crime? Approaching Jesus, "She said, 'Grant that one of these two sons of mine may sit at your right and the other at your left in your kingdom'" (Matthew 20:21). And while this may seem harmless enough at first glance, let's consider the context. In the preceding verses, Jesus shared some rather disturbing news with His disciples.

> "We are going up to Jerusalem, and the Son of Man will be deliv-ered over to the chief priests and the teachers of the law. They will condemn him to death and will hand him over to the Gentiles to be mocked and flogged and crucified. On the third day he will be raised to life!" (Matthew 20:18-19 NIV)

Jesus has just foreshadowed His death. And yet, along with their mother, James and John saw an opportunity for advancement.

"So, Jesus, after you're raised to life and you establish this new kingdom, are you looking for a right-hand and left-hand man?"

The Son of God had just shared the brutal death that He would endure, and two of Jesus' closest followers skip right over it to consider their own glory.

Now, when the other ten disciples heard of this, they were livid, but not for the reason you'd think. We'd hope that they'd chastise James and John for their insensitive request or their glory-seeking appetite. Truth be told, they were mad because James and John asked first.

Unfortunately, this response resembles the heart of so many. If we're being honest, it often reflects our own hearts. Rather than asking God how we can serve Him, we grow fixated on how God can serve us. We don't knock over the blocks; we stack them up and ask God for more blocks. But Jesus is very clear on His expectations both for those early disciples and for us. Jesus paints them a picture of how the world works, where rulers and officials seek authority to oppress those they lead. And then Jesus said:

> "Not so with you. Instead, whoever wants to become great among you must be your servant, and whoever wants to be first must be your slave—just as the Son of Man did not come to be served, but to serve, and to give his life as a ransom for many." (Matthew 20:26-28)

Jesus was trying to paint a different picture for them. "My Kingdom works quite different from this kingdom. If you want to lead in mine, you must be the first servant." It's picking a fight worthy of your life and then knocking over the blocks. It's dying up front so that you can really live. It's choosing to live for a higher purpose.

PICK UP THE TOWEL AND SERVE

Jesus was the master teacher. When Jesus died so that others can live again, His very life became a metaphor. Before He was arrested, beaten, flogged, and crucified, Jesus ate the Passover meal with His disciples. As they partook in this memorial celebration, Jesus taught them how this meal was a foreshadowing of His death. "This bread is a symbol of my body, which will be broken for you. In the same way, this wine is like my blood, which will be poured out on your behalf" (Matthew 26:26, 28 paraphrased).

Once again, Jesus was teaching them about His ultimate act of service and the kind of life they would be expected to live.

Then, this grand act was given one more visual representation. Though before I unfold what Jesus did, I want to highlight what Jesus knew. In John 13, the author writes that Jesus was fully aware that God had given Him all power and authority in heaven and on earth. If you had all power, what would you do? I could quickly come up with a list of no less than one hundred things—at least half of which would serve my desires—likely placing me on a beautiful island with a hammock, a light breeze, and a stellar view. But that's the opposite of what Jesus does.

The story continues, "so he got up from the meal, took off his outer clothing, and wrapped a towel around his waist. After that, he poured water into a basin and began to wash his disciples' feet, drying them with the towel that was wrapped around him" (John 13:4-5 NIV). In full view of the power and authority granted Him, Jesus didn't serve Himself. He served those in front of Him. Jesus knocked over the blocks and He picked up a towel. The Son of God, the Creator, the Lord of heaven and earth, became a servant.

Soon, Jesus would be massacred beyond recognition. Rather than seek His own comfort and gain, Jesus wanted to drive home a central message to the people who would carry His message to the corners of the earth: "'Now that I, your Lord and Teacher, have washed your feet, you also should wash one another's feet. I have set you an example that you should do as I have done for you'" (John 13:14-15 NIV).

We serve the Great Servant. We follow the footsteps of our Master. We knock over the blocks, and we pick up the towel. We carry our corner of the mat, and we rip open the roof. We do whatever it takes to get people to the healing hands of Jesus. It isn't about the name on our jersey; it's about the Name that is above every other name. We don't lose heart because we know the heart of the One we follow. As we do whatever it takes, our faith will make a difference. We believe Jesus when He said, "'Now that you know these things, you will be blessed if you do them'" (John 13:17 NIV).

QUESTIONS for TRANSFORMATION

1. As you think about the events of your life most weeks, are you stacking up the blocks against the people around you? What steps can you take to knock over the blocks and live more for the people in your life?

2. When you think about serving God, what actions do you hold in high regard? Do you seek opportunities for recognition, or is it about God's love reaching others?

3. In what ways has fear held you back from life-giving actions toward others? Going forward, what are some selfless ways that you can help others to encounter God's love?

4. When you're tempted to throw in the towel, how will you remember to pick it up and serve others like Jesus?

"Oh, how great peace and quietness should he possess, that would cut off all vain anxiety . . . and would place all his confidence in God."

—THOMAS À KEMPIS[16]

CHAPTER 9

TRUST BEYOND COMFORT

God literally stopped me in my tracks one morning.

I was going for a run in our Mississippi neighborhood. Perhaps the gasping for breath makes me feel closer to my Maker, but I love to pray when I run. In fact, I can distinctly remember two times when God almost knocked me over with a whisper, and both times, I was finishing up a run. On both occasions, I was wrestling with God, and I limped away similar to Jacob at Peniel.

On this muggy Mississippi run, I was sensing that God was again doing a new thing that would likely require a move in our family's future. Honestly, I was grieved at the prospect. As you can read, we've moved *a lot*. I loved our church and what it meant to our family. I loved my role, and I had worked so hard. I felt so blessed by God to be entrusted with such an honorable position. And honestly, I didn't want to give up our home. Seriously, we hadn't owned a home in more than six years, and this was our dream house.

While I ran and shared with God why His plans didn't fit with my plans, I began to sense a lack of faith in my heart. *God, you can't ask me to do this*, I cried out. *I don't think I can do this again.* As I shared my concerns, I rounded the final corner of my run at the top of a hill. At the opposite end of the street and down the hill was our house, the dream home we'd come to love. *God, you gave us this. Please don't take it away*, I pleaded. Having spent years without a home to call our own, we did believe that God had blessed us with this beautiful house.

And that's when God stopped me in my tracks. His whisper caught me like a mighty rush of wind.

"Chad, is this as far as you'll trust Me?"

He even used my first name. God couldn't have been any clearer. He wanted to raise my faith and my trust, but old faith couldn't take me there. I especially sensed that God wanted to expand our family's impact and responsibility. However, it would require letting go of what God had previously provided to take us to this new place of trust and impact. God is less concerned about our material possessions and far more concerned with our spiritual influence. Don't hear me wrong—I do believe that God provides and even wants to bless His children as they faithfully follow Him. I have endless stories of how I've seen God provide for us and so many others. But I also believe that God's highest aim is to develop character within us that overflows into making a difference for the Kingdom. His blessings are how He expands our opportunities to get there.

Faith must be fought for. Some days, you'll wake up faith-filled, ready to take on whatever challenges await. On those days, it's almost as though you don't even see the obstacles, or at least you don't fully grasp their size, because all you can see is the strength of God. But on other days, the gravity of earthly realities will weigh heavily on you. For me, it felt like I was sleep-walking, only to awaken and realize how far out on the limb I've walked.

And yet, there's something beautiful about this moment if you'll lean into God, for it's there that you'll discover greater levels of trust. God loves what He gets to unveil to you in these situations, and it's generally more of

His presence. I've never found that old faith is enough for today's challenges. Sure, old faith has memory, which can inspire you to continue trusting. But new challenges will require new trust.

STAND IN THE RIVER

So, how far will you trust? God's ultimate goal for your life is not merely for you to have a story about that one time you had faith and God moved mightily. Obviously, I love a good faith story—this book is full of them. However, the best faith stories are still being written, right now, in the present. God wants you to walk in the midst of miracles, not just to simply remember one that happened years ago. Tell the stories both to remind you of God's faithfulness and to instigate action in others around you. But be willing to walk in a story here today!

This was God's message to Israel as Joshua assumed leadership. A new generation was now responsible for faithfully following God. They grew up hearing stories of how God led their ancestors to walk across dry ground where the Red Sea's violent waves had once reigned. As Moses led the people to exit Egypt, he raised his staff before the mighty waters. Rather than the waves crashing against the shore, the water stood at attention as the people of God walked through. Then, that generation passed away. They all died without seeing the promised land; well, everyone but Joshua and Caleb. Once they crossed over, their faith dwindled, and they no longer believed that the God who parted the sea was able to push back their enemies. Rather than inheriting their God-given land, they roamed nearly four decades as nomads in the desert.

Now it was time for their children to display their own faith, demonstrating that they would not repeat the same mistakes of their posterity. But new territory required new faith. As the two men that remained faith-filled in the midst of their faithless tribesmen, Joshua and Caleb would lead the charge.

And the Lord said to Joshua, "Today I will begin to exalt you in the eyes of all Israel, so they may know that I am with you as I was with Moses. Tell the priests who carry the ark of the covenant: 'When you reach the edge of the Jordan's waters, go and stand in the river.'" (Joshua 3:7-8 NIV)

Moses stood on the shore and raised his staff. Now, the priests would have to "go and stand in the river." It would not be enough to stand safely on shore and wait for God to move. This time, they'd have to get in the water.

It may seem like a subtle difference, but how often do we expect God to move in our lives exactly as He has in the past? And in the waiting, we become paralyzed with fear, certain our old faith will be enough. It may seem like a small change, but I assure you that the priests didn't feel this way.

So when the people broke camp to cross the Jordan, the priests carrying the ark of the covenant went ahead of them. Now the Jordan is at *flood stage* all during harvest. Yet as soon as the priests who carried that ark reached the Jordan and their feet touched the water's edge, the water from upstream stopped flowing. It piled up in a heap a great distance away . . . The priests who carried the ark of the covenant of the Lord stopped in the middle of the Jordan and stood on dry ground, while all Israel passed by until the whole nation had completed the crossing on dry ground. (Joshua 3:14-17 NIV, emphasis added)

It's believed that the ark of the covenant weighed close to two hundred pounds. At its normal flow, the Jordan River is somewhere between three to ten feet in depth, and between ninety to a hundred feet in width.[17]

Add to this the fact that the crossing was taking place while the Jordan was at flood stage, and now the crossing was no less miraculous than what transpired a generation ago. But they couldn't stand on the shore; the priests had to get in the water. Moreover, they held the ark on their shoulders while the entire nation, several hundred thousand people, crossed over. While the task was daunting, they got a front-row seat to the miraculous. Had they stayed comfortably on the shore, not only would the priests have forfeited their chance to participate in God's plan, so too would another generation have surrendered their chance to inherit God's miracle. That day, the people of Israel became a nation moving into a land, and it didn't happen waiting on the shore. They had to get in the river.

MOMENTARY AMNESIA

Living in the wake of great miracles, Elijah would have grown up hearing the stories of Moses and Joshua. His ancestors would have handed down the great stories in hopes of passing on great faith. But as the great prophet, Elijah himself would have firsthand experience, witnessing story after story of God's extraordinary miracles. He didn't need someone to tell him that God is powerful; he saw it with his own eyes. And yet, even the faith of the great Elijah would fail. This means that Elijah's a great person to help us remember that failure isn't final. Even one of the greatest prophets of the Old Testament found the end of his trust in God, but he didn't stay there.

If you go back to 1 Kings 17, you'll see Elijah tell King Ahab that there would be a three-year drought. Ahab was the king of Israel, but he did not follow God. As a result, the whole land was receiving punishment. Three years later in 1 Kings 18, God sent Elijah back to Ahab to say that the drought would end; rain was coming. God wanted Israel to know who makes it rain and who holds it back, and Elijah was God's instrument on display. He told Ahab to gather all 850 of his false prophets and meet him on Mount Carmel. Important to note—Elijah will stand on a couple of mountains during our discussion, and it's critical to understand the role that each of them will play. When you think of Mount Carmel, I want you to think of Elijah at his best. Got it locked in? Mount Carmel equals Elijah at his best. Perfect.

Then Elijah told the 850 false prophets to build an altar and wait for fire to fall from heaven to burn up the sacrifice. The only problem was nothing happened. Elijah mocked them. He said, "Maybe your gods are thinking, or maybe they're traveling, perhaps they're sleeping." My favorite taunt is when Elijah suggests that maybe their gods were going to the bathroom. I'm serious! You can't make this stuff up. They called out to their false gods for hours, they danced around their altar, they even cut themselves with swords, but nothing happened.

Then Elijah built his altar, and he poured jar after jar of water on top of his altar. He wanted it to be clear only God could light up this sacrifice. Then he stopped everything, and Elijah began to pray mightily.

> "O Lord, God of Abraham, Isaac, and Israel, let it be known this day that you are God in Israel, and that I am your servant, and that I have done all these things at your word. Answer me, O Lord, answer me, that this people may know that you, O Lord, are God, and that you have turned their hearts back." Then the fire of the Lord fell and consumed the burnt offering and the wood and the stones and the dust, and licked up the water that was in the trench. And when all the people saw it, they fell on their faces and said, "The Lord, he is God; the Lord, he is God." (1 Kings 18:36-39)

Soon, the heavens opened up and a great rain fell upon the land for the first time in three years. God moved mightily, and he used Elijah as His representative.

On Mount Carmel, Elijah was at the top of his game. In 1 Kings 17-18, Elijah cannot be stopped. He performed one miracle after another. But in Chapter 19, he fell on his face. He went from unstoppable to missing in action. Seemingly overnight, the guy that stared down the king and 850 prophets was running like a coward.

Here's what happened: Soon after the rain came, Ahab went back to the palace and told his wife, Jezebel, what Elijah did. She was livid, and she put a bounty on Elijah's head. She swore to stop at nothing until he was dead. When Elijah heard of her plot, he just got up and ran for an entire day into the wilderness. Earlier, Elijah was calling down fire from heaven. Now look at his next prayer: "It is enough; now, O LORD, take away my life . . ." (1 Kings 19:4). He literally prayed to die. *It's enough God. I've got nothing left. Just kill me now.*

What? What happened to the false-prophet-slaying, take-no-junk-off-nobody, miracle-performing Elijah? In the midst of the fear and trauma of being hunted, Elijah acquired momentary amnesia. He'd forgotten his standing with God, and he'd forgotten the goodness and power of God. But honestly, this is what I love about Elijah's story.

Elijah was a hero and a giant of our faith. But giants fall hard. We too have our giant moments, our 1 Kings 17-18 on Mount Carmel, if you will. But we also have our failures. Moments when we wake up and realize how far we've walked out on the limb. Times when our trust comes to its end. We all have a 1 Kings 19 when things are not going our way. Maybe we failed or we just feel like a failure. For Elijah, his failure followed his greatest triumph, which makes the sting of his downfall all the more painful.

GOD STILL LOVES YOU EVEN ON YOUR WORST DAYS

So, how do you get past your past? How do you forgive yourself? Where do you find the grace when you feel behind in life? Elijah went from having his best day to having his worst day. But if Elijah were standing here today, he'd tell you what he would come to learn in time: "God still loves you even on your worst days." Maybe you need to hear your heavenly Father say those words to you today: "I still love you even on your worst days."[18]

115

Perhaps one of the most important lessons that we can learn from Elijah's distrust in God's faithfulness during this difficult season of life is you can't disappoint God. Let me say it again: You can't disappoint God. To be sure, Elijah was disappointed in himself. He was God's mighty prophet. And yet, when he faced death, he tucked his tail and ran. When he finally sat down after running for his life, he was so overcome with grief that he asked to die. He was disappointed in himself, and thus, he imagined God was disappointed with him too. But there's an important lesson here: Don't project your feelings onto God. Our disappointment arises when our experience falls short of our expectations. But nothing catches God by surprise, so nothing falls short of His expectations. God isn't shocked by your mistake because God knows you. He knows you inside and out. He knows you from beginning to end, and He loves you completely.[19]

Moreover, when you feel like you've run out of faith, remember that God knows what you need and provides. I know that sounds cliché, but lock this in your heart. When you are in your moments of greatest need, you'll be tempted to do it all in your own strength and find solutions that are less than God's best. In those moments, remember God knows what you need and provides.

Elijah was alone, and his energy was gone. He had nothing left in the tank. But remember, Elijah was on his own because he ran away. He chose to be alone. Truth is, when we fail, we allow our shame to drive us away from people. Also true is this: Often when we want to be around people the least is when we need them the most. This is an old trick by the devil to isolate you in your shame. Don't fall for it. The Bible actually teaches us that when we open up ourselves with other followers of Jesus, it brings healing in our lives. This is exactly why doing life in community is so important. In the wake of seasons like COVID-19, we all need community more than ever before. Elijah was alone with nothing, and he was zapped of strength. God sent an angel to Elijah's side to provide food, water, and rest. Soon, he was strong enough to walk 250 miles over forty days. God knows what we need, and God provides.

WHY DOES GOD WHISPER?

Next, Elijah arrived at Mount Horeb, and he hid away in a cave. Mount Carmel showed Elijah at his best, but Mount Horeb displays Elijah at his worst. He'd been on the run for weeks. No longer full of faith, he was overcome with fear.

Elijah's struggle is a great reminder that when we're empty, you must let God fill you up. Do you realize that the God of the universe loves to meet and connect with *you*? God's favorite thing is to talk with *you*. God speaks to Elijah and tells him to come out of the cave. Soon after, a mighty rushing wind passes by, but God wasn't in the wind. Soon, an earthquake shook the foundations of the mountain, but God wasn't in the earthquake. Then, a fire fell from heaven, much like the fire that consumed the altar back on Mount Carmel, but God wasn't in the fire this time.

Just like the priests standing on the shore of the Jordan, it would have been natural for Elijah to expect God to show up like He did before. But God usually meets us in new and unexpected ways. God wants to have a new and fresh experience *with* you because God wants to build new and fresh faith *in* you. Then, after all the wind and shaking and fires ceased, God spoke to Elijah in a whisper. Elijah had done work *for* God, but he hadn't slowed down to enjoy time *with* God.

Think about the last time you were at a big party where it was super loud, which therefore required everyone to speak loudly. The room probably wasn't made for great acoustics, so sound is bouncing off of every wall. You probably couldn't hear one person over the other; there was just a noisy dissonance. But if someone leaned over to you in the middle of it and whispered, they'd cup their hand and speak in a different frequency. You'd lean in to listen, and even with all the noise, you'd hear them.

Why does God whisper? God won't compete with all the other noise, and He won't shout to be heard. God whispers to be experienced. When

God whispers, you lean in. God whispers because God is close. God isn't trying to add one more thing to your life; God desires to become your life. God wants to move to the center, to be your first and your last, to be your constant guide and companion. And God doesn't have to shout because He isn't far away. He's right here with you.[20]

FAILURE ISN'T FINAL

On Mount Carmel, the mighty prophet was triumphant, but on Mount Horeb, Elijah was human. Your faith will fail, but your failure isn't final. When you turn to God, He always has the last word. There will be moments when we throw in the towel on ourselves, frustrated that our trust has run out. But know this: God never loses faith in what He sees in you. Sure, Elijah had fallen, but in the artistic hands of God, failure can be an opportunity. If we leverage our mistakes, failure becomes the open door for us to experience God's steadfast strength in us. Do you know what God did next with Elijah? He gave him another mission. Why? Because failure isn't final. Elijah may have failed, but God didn't give up on him. God told Elijah to get back on mission because God had work for him to do.

Elijah's faith soared on Mount Carmel when Ahab and the 850 false prophets watched as God showed up and showed off. Elijah's faith tumbled when he sat alone in the cave on Mount Horeb. But let this important truth sink deep into your soul: God loved Elijah just as much on Mount Horeb as he did back on Mount Carmel. And God loves you on your worst days too. God loves you just as much in your failures as He does in your successes. God's love isn't fleeting. God's love isn't based on your performance. God won't desert you when you're at your lowest. God will find you, pick you up, dust you off, and send you back in the game even when you throw in the towel on yourself. God will not give up on you. God loves you. God put purpose in you. Failure isn't final; it's often the door you'll walk through on the way to God's biggest plans for your life.

UNEXPECTED GIFTS

Katie and I married quite young. I turned twenty just four days before our wedding day, and she was eighteen, just a month and a half after her high school graduation. Like I said, we were quite young. So while it was tough, there was a gift in it. All those challenges you face in the various phases of life, especially in your early twenties—we got to experience them together. Just a year into our marriage, we moved to Mansfield, Ohio, which is about an hour north of Columbus and an hour south of Cleveland. We were the first ones in each of our families to move away, which meant we had no blueprint for how to do it. Add to this fact that Mansfield, Ohio, is one of the most beautiful and underrated corners of the country, but only about two months of the year. The other ten months are cold, overcast, and snowy. And did I mention cold and snowy?

I was doing a student ministry internship while continuing my under-graduate studies. For an eighteen-year-old, Katie found a great job. Sadly, the oral surgeon that she worked for was diagnosed with cancer and suddenly had to close down his practice. As we approached our first Christmas in northern Ohio, the combination of cold weather, no family, and extremely low income was beginning to wear on us. Since we were in ministry, we were present at the church for the Christmas Eve services, which also meant that we wouldn't be with family.

Heading into the holidays, our spirits were low, and we were lonely. That's when another couple invited us over for Christmas Eve dinner following the worship services. Brad and Judi were empty nesters, yet they remained highly involved in the student ministry. Along with other young couples, we experienced a joy-filled evening with lots of laughter, began lifelong friendships, and enjoyed some incredible food. It was a wonderful evening that became an unexpected gift in the midst of a wilderness season for us. It was a vivid reminder of God's goodness and faithfulness to us throughout every season of our lives.

Elijah also had unexpected gifts in the midst of his own wilderness wanderings. He went from the mountain of triumph to the valley of failure. But Elijah learned that while we appreciate God on the mountaintop, we get to experience God in the valley. Often, some of our great victories will be followed by epic setbacks. This will be a shock to your system, but let it also be a reminder to you that your deep needs can become unexpected gifts if they drive you to rely on God. You will never regret depending on God for your source of peace and wisdom.

Elijah had quite the journey. He had stared down an evil king and called down a three-year drought. While on the run, he was fed by ravens and raised the life of a dead child. He stood down 850 false prophets and called down fire from heaven. Then, he called down the rain, and God brought a torrent. Despite all that he had seen and done, when Jezebel came after him, he was undone. One angry woman, and Elijah was on the run! Do you remember what he prayed? "'I have had enough, Lord'" (1 Kings 19:5 NLT).

I suspect that most of us have had our own *enough* moments. You're trying to raise the kids right, but you wonder why it doesn't seem to be working. You can't possibly face that situation at work. One more day will surely do you in. Financially, the car breaks down, the toilet overflows, and a kid puts a Lego up their nose. Like Elijah, it's usually a straw that breaks the camel's back. It can be something small or something big, but it's that final weight and you have had enough.

When you reach this place, where will you turn? Perhaps the better question is, *who* will you turn to? In our culture today, it's become a badge of honor to say that you're tired or exhausted. But it's important not to confuse physical needs with spiritual ones. If we're physically tired, a nap and a snack will do the trick. When we're spiritually drained, we need a touch from God.

Understanding the difference between physical needs and spiritual needs is an essential tool for a follower of Jesus. Most people assume recreation alone is what they need, so they break from the wrong things. Assuming their family is tired, they stop going to church, stop showing up to small group and take an undefined break from serving. People take more weekend trips and sign up the kids for more activities. These aren't inherently bad, but they're the equivalent of loading up on every pain reliever at the pharmacy when you really needed to visit the eye doctor. Not only did you vastly misdiagnose the problem, but you're also hurting yourself. You might be numbing some pain, but you're creating other problems.

What happened to Elijah so often happens to us. We get spiritually drained and physically tired, and then we forget what God taught us in our last challenging season. Therein, we must learn to remember in seasons of depletion what God taught us in seasons of abundance. What's true on the mountain is true in the valley. We are made to serve God and depend on Him. We can't abandon the things of God when we're drained and tired; we must lean in and experience the unexpected gifts.

If you feel like Elijah—at the end of your rope—it's probably *been* time to get into God's presence. Elijah's tiredness and depletion meant that he could bring nothing to God; he only received from God. If you're in a similar place, that's fine with God. Maybe you feel stuck in a job and you're trying to figure out what to do next. Or you want to buy a house, but you're unsure if you should continue renting because there's lots of uncertainty. You might be thinking, "When is this relationship going to move forward? I can't stay stuck in this place." Whether you feel alone, lost, or disoriented, it's time to get into God's presence. When the angel of God touched Elijah, things began to turn. God stands ready to move in your life too. If you'll allow the valley season to drive you to God, you'll discover unexpected gifts from Him. You'll discover that God's presence will be the only present you've needed.

NEW WINE, NEW WINESKINS

God was ready to do something new in Elijah, and Elijah wasn't sure if he could climb another mountain. But did you notice the other name for Mount Horeb? It's the Mountain of God. God was ready to turn Elijah's worst moment into his greatest. But a new work required new movement. What God wanted to do in and through Elijah couldn't take place at Carmel. It had to begin at Horeb.

Jesus described this type of spiritual movement with a metaphor: "'And no one puts new wine into old wineskins. If he does, the wine will burst the skins—and the wine is destroyed, and so are the skins. But new wine is for fresh wineskins'" (Mark 2:22). Often, when God brings about a new work, He first will bring an adjustment. For Elijah, it was the transfer to Horeb. For Peter, it was learning to follow Jesus with wisdom and passion. Like we discovered in Chapter Two, it's changing the playlist from lies we've believed to God's truths we must grab hold of.

In distress, Elijah had believed many lies. He thought he would be murdered. He felt certain he was alone. He had decided that his best days were behind. In truth, seven thousand faithful people remained. Soon he'd anoint his successor. And not only would he not be murdered—Elijah never died. In time, he'd be swept up by God in a whirlwind with chariots and horses of fire; he would literally go out in a blaze of glory. The stirring he felt was a new wave of God's grace coming to Israel. New wine required new wineskins.

New wineskins can look different for each person in every season. Like Elijah, there may be a physical move involved that births a new ministry.

It may mean a new role, either as an employee or as a volunteer within an organization. It may mean leading differently right where you are. New wineskins can be an entirely new perspective of how you follow Jesus in the spaces and places you already inhabit.

For me, new wineskins begin in the presence of Jesus each morning. I open up the scriptures with a Bible reading plan. I pray and ask God to open my eyes and ears to His living and active Word. I ask the Holy Spirit to make my spirit sensitive to God's voice. The God that whispered on Mount Horeb whispers today. Jesus who met with Peter on the shore desires to meet with you today. The Holy Spirit that moved in the early church is moving in your midst today. As you daily cultivate a practice of being present with God, you'll become new wineskin for the new wine God desires to pour out today.

HOW FAR WILL YOU TRUST?

For us, new wine was establishing a new outpost for the Gospel to be proclaimed, and the new wineskin was Indianapolis, Indiana. We had bought our dream home and planted our roots in Jackson, Mississippi, but God was speaking clearly. He didn't bring us to Jackson as a destination; it was a preparation for what was coming. During our first two years at Pinelake, while I had the privilege of leading one of the largest church campuses in the country, God was building a spiritual fortification *within* me. And while it was hard work, I was content to stay where God had brought us, but that wasn't God's intention.

At the recommendation of our church's leadership, we began asking God what He had for our lives, and specifically, was He asking us to launch a new church in Indianapolis? Being completely honest, I loved living in the South, and I loved leading within an existing organization. My Pastor, Chip Henderson, had encouraged us to consider creating a new work in our home state. No one was more surprised than me when four months later I marched into his office and stated, "Yes! That's exactly what God is calling us to do."

Katie and I had prayed and talked, but it was God's stirring that led the way. Through times of prayer, worship, and reading Scripture, we had become fully convinced that God was moving us back home. I'll never forget my pastor's response: "Chad, I sense that this is what the Spirit is leading you to do, and I believe we're supposed to be in your corner." Prayer, worship, Scripture, and now people had confirmed it. In the subsequent days, more people would confirm and even make commitments to join us.

On September 10, 2017, we launched Echo Church on the west side of Indianapolis in Avon, Indiana. In the years that followed, thousands of people worshipped with us, over five hundred people began a life-saving relationship with Jesus; we partnered with local agencies to fight domestic violence, homelessness, and hunger; through international partnerships, we touched five continents; and we helped launch more than four hundred new churches. I could have kept my dream home and my status as a large-church pastor, but I would have forfeited the opportunity to join God on mission, and this beautiful new work wouldn't have been established.

And four and a half years later, God asked us to trust Him with a new step. In April 2022, we merged our young church with a church 185 years old to launch a new campus. Ordinarily, this might seem like new wine inside of a old wineskin. However, this church has consistently made bold choices to become new, including a new location and a new building, a name change, new leaders, and updated methods. Therein, it's actually new wine inside of a 185-year-old wineskin that continues to renew itself. This faith step was one of the most difficult decisions I ever made in ministry. As I'm writing this, the story is still being written. In a short amount of time, God has used that step of faith to produce four additional congregations. Somehow God is producing new wine and multiplying seed at the same time.

How far will you trust God? I regularly remind myself to dare to live *God's* dreams for my life. Yes, God will bring blessings your way, but you cannot cling to them. Rather, they are vessels for impact and opportunity. To a world watching and wondering, "Do Christians really trust God with their lives?" our decisions preach a message that our words never can. I pray that you'll trust beyond comfort.

QUESTIONS for TRANSFORMATION

1. How have past successes or failures kept you from trusting God with your future?

2. How is God currently whispering to you, and how will you trust Him fully with what's ahead?

3. List some of the unexpected gifts that God has brought into your life in the midst of difficult seasons.

4. New wine requires new wineskins. How are you actively opening yourself to what God wants to do in and through your life?

ATTRIBUTE 4
MADE *to* REFLECT

Grappling Greed, Pruning Pride, Extinguishing Entitlement

"And endurance develops strength of character, and character strengthens our confident hope of salvation. And this hope will not lead to disappointment. For we know how dearly God loves us, because he has given us the Holy Spirit to fill our hearts with his love."

—Romans 5:4-5 NLT

"Cultivate the habit of being grateful for every good thing that comes to you . . . And because all things have contributed to your advancement, you should include all things in your gratitude."

——RALPH WALDO EMERSON[21]

"We make a living by what we get, but we make a life by what we give."

——WINSTON CHURCHILL[22]

CHAPTER 10

UNLOCK YOUR FUTURE

As we embarked on Christmas holiday travel in 2004, a severe winter storm swept across the Ohio River Valley. We were in north-central Ohio, attempting to make our way to west-central Indiana. Under good conditions, the trip could be made in a little more than four hours. In this instance, the combination of historic weather and the influx of holiday travelers resulted in more than twelve white-knuckle hours. Two lanes on interstates had narrowed to two barely visible tire tracks, and the range of visibility dwindled to the taillights of the car directly in front of us. This was made all the more heart-racing as lead cars would skid on ice and drift into the quickly forming snowbank at the road's edge.

As we approached Dayton, Ohio, state troopers had shut down a stretch of Interstate 70 and directed traffic to the south side of the city. As we worked our way back north and through the city, conditions only worsened. Cars that had stalled in traffic hours earlier became hazards to avoid in the middle of a lane. Plow trucks made one path that weaved amongst lanes, between abandoned cars, and beside snow embankments. It felt like driving through a wintry Armageddon.

Miraculously making our way through the icy gauntlet, we attempted to merge back onto Interstate 70. Hoping that we had made it past the road closure, we were looking for the on-ramp amidst a heavy construction zone. We tried to find and follow signs, merged onto a ramp, and suddenly found our car heading east. If you're keeping track of our coordinates, we had taken the wrong ramp and were now heading back in the direction of the initial road closure. Soon, we saw a dozen large plow trucks, closely followed by a flurry of Ohio State Troopers with their lights swirling and then trailed by what seemed like an endless river of headlights. When we finally reached an exit to turnaround, we were now behind a flood of holiday travelers. Unable to merge back onto the interstate, we resigned to sleeping for several hours in a gas station parking lot.

Ultimately, we had gone in the exact opposite direction of what we wanted. The storm and the road construction combined to distract and confuse, leaving us stranded at an exit and adding hours to our already-exhausting trip. In life and leadership, storms and distractions are inevitable. Without a set of God-honoring values, a lack of character will drive you in the exact opposite direction of your most-desired destination.

The core conviction of this book is not only that you are made for more, but that you are *made*. You are designed, cultivated, crafted, created by a Creator, on purpose, for a purpose. As we've already learned, you are made to live fully, made with divine purpose, and made for impact in the world. In this section, you'll discover that you are made to mirror the Creator.

At the beginning of Creation, and at the creation of you, Father, Son, and Holy Spirit proclaimed, "Let us make them in our own image" (See Genesis 1:26-28). As we grow our character, the person we see in the mirror reflects more and more the One that fashioned us.

To be clear, values have already been at the core of this book. We've talked about how honor propels a young leader into their future. We've seen how radical faith can place us inside of God's desire for our lives.

Perseverance will fortify you for the arduous journey of unearthing a life worth living. Self-giving courage will catapult you into a fight worthy of your days. In this chapter and the next, we'll discover how gratitude and generosity, integrity, and wholeness mirror our Creator and guide us into the future God has designed for us.

WHERE DO YOU WANT TO GO?

One of my favorite things to do is travel. And because of stories like the one above, I typically prefer to fly. However, while my beautiful bride Katie enjoys the destinations, she hates to fly. So, when I come up with great travel ideas, it's important for me to think about how we'll get there. Plan a trip with me for a moment.

If I want to take Katie to London from Indianapolis, I won't first travel to L.A. I'm not looking for flights out of Seattle. I'm looking for the shortest and smoothest path to our desired destination. So often, while people have a vague idea of where they want to go in life, they have no plan for how to get there. In fact, I would suggest that a lot of people are trying to get to London by way of Alaska. Their priorities and choices are sabotaging where they truly want to go with their lives. Specifically, choices made from a place of entitlement and greed will place you on a road going in the exact opposite direction.

Where do you want to go? If the tires on your car are even slightly misaligned, your car won't go in the direction that you want. Chiropractors will tell you that if your spine is misaligned, your body won't do what you ask. If your priorities are misaligned, your life won't end up where you want to go.

I recently spent time with a leadership coach, and we did a powerful exercise. He had me think about where I want my life to go in the next twenty years. I began asking myself: What do I want to be doing? What do

I want to have accomplished? In essence, where do I want to go? Then, we started working backwards. To get there, I must carefully choose my priorities for the next ten years, the next five years, and the next twelve months.

What about you? What do you want to accomplish? What kind of impact do you want to have on the world? What are the top priorities for your household? And if you can picture where you want to go, you next need to think about where you'll begin. Because where you start matters.

You must start with your character and the values that will drive your life. Gratitude will extinguish entitlement that sabotages you, and generosity will lead you to grapple greed that holds you back. Moreover, gratitude reflects the heart of Jesus (See Luke 22:19), and generosity embodies the character of our giving Father (See John 3:16). If you desire to unlock the future destined for you, gratitude and generosity are the keys to getting there.

EXTINGUISH ENTITLEMENT

Sometimes God will select interesting moments to grab our attention.

In this instance, I was driving to Bob Evans in Mansfield, Ohio, to meet a former boss and mentor. Thomas took a risk and invested in me while still in my early twenties. We were grabbing breakfast, but this wasn't a cordial gathering. I had learned that he shared things about me during a reference check, and the insights weren't very kind. I was hurt and angry, and I wanted to confront him.

While driving to breakfast, I was praying with my serious voice: "God, who does he think he is? He never really gave me a chance. Besides, we haven't talked in two years. He doesn't know me now. God, help me have the wisdom and courage to tell him what I think of him and *his* leadership."

And that's when God had heard enough and decided to silence my noise with a whisper: "Chad, I want you to tell him, 'Thank you.'"

What? You can't be serious, I replied. *"Thank you"? Why would I tell him "thank you" when he said these things about me?*

And that's when God dropped the mic.

"Because you never thanked him for investing in you."

My mind began to race.

Surely, I did, I thought to myself. *There must have been a moment early in the journey when I told him "thank you." There must have been.* Except, I couldn't remember a single time when I expressed my gratitude for what he had done for Katie and me.

Just a year into our marriage, I had applied for a Junior High Pastor position and Thomas was the Director of Student Ministries. I was young, inexperienced, and I didn't have a degree. I didn't get the job, but because he wanted to invest in me, Thomas offered me a three-year internship where I could learn while earning my undergraduate degree.

I thought back to those early days of ministry together, and I realized that it was highly likely I had not expressed gratitude. This leader offered me a three-year internship. Who offers anyone an internship that long? Let me answer the question for you: no one! When Katie and I moved and had no money, Thomas sent a few guys with a truck to help pick up our stuff. When we had dreams but no next steps, he said, "We've got you!"

When I arrived and sat in the booth across from Thomas, who was roughly twice my age, I asked if I could share something before we began.

"I know we've got some things to work out, but I need to say something that is long overdue. *Thank you* for investing in me. And I'm sorry that I didn't say it sooner."

Tears began to well up in his eyes, and he said, "Chad, when I walked out the door, my wife said to me, 'Tell me if he says 'thank you.''"

What I realize now and couldn't understand then is that when a mature leader selects a young leader to work with, they invest so much of their life into them. It's real, it's raw, it's personal, and it's often thankless. In that moment, I think he was somewhat emotional because he felt appreciated, but I think he was mostly emotional because he felt as though his deposit in my life was beginning to bear fruit. A sense of entitlement had held me back from optimal learning and impact, and it kept me from a rich relationship with this generous leader. Gratitude not only unlocked our relationship, but it also began to awaken my character and grow my desire to be guided by a set of God-honoring values.

GRATITUDE

Gratitude is the antiseptic of entitlement, and it's a prime doorway into God's favor. I thought I deserved the full-time role at the church in Ohio, which prevented me from seeing the opportunities that had been given to me and displaying gratitude. You will never go wrong with gratitude. It opens the heart to see blessing in every challenge, honor in every person, and hope in every situation.

Paul says to "Give thanks in all circumstances . . ." (1 Thessalonians 5:18). The psalmist writes, "This is the day that the Lord has made; lets us rejoice and be glad in it" (Psalm 118:24). James reminds us that "Every good gift and every perfect gift is from above . . ." (James 1:17). Gratitude reflects a heart with great awareness of God's goodness, abundance, and gracious heart towards His children. Entitlement and greed reflect the heart of God's enemy, Satan, who wanted more status and glory in heaven. A role in God's Kingdom wasn't enough; he wanted it all (Isaiah 14:12-15). When we live with gratitude, God's heart is opened toward us, and His favor rests on us.

If you find that your heart has hardened toward others, especially those in leadership over you, ask yourself about the level of your gratitude. I promise you their leadership role is far more complex than you realize. Of course, complexity doesn't negate their responsibility to lead well. But your responsibility to live with gratitude isn't negated by their quality of leadership. Your responsibility is to God. When Paul directs us to live with gratitude in all situations, there is no disclaimer and no exceptions to the rule. Gratitude isn't about others; it's you. It's about your heart. When you lead with gratitude, you are magnetic to God's favor because you're reflecting His heart.

GRAPPLING GREED

Most people assume that other people are greedy. Greedy people, they reckon, are already rich and just desire to have more. And if you don't start out rich, well then you can't be greedy. Of course, greed has far more to do with your heart posture than your financial portfolio. Sometimes greed is about gaining more and more. Often, greed is less about acquiring and more about gripping tightly what you already have.

Entitlement convinces you that you deserve more than you've earned. Greed is believing the lie that what you earned actually belongs to you. In truth, what you have is a result of where you started in life, the faculties given you by a benevolent God, and the structures that you inhabit. Hard work and ingenuity are incredibly important, but they are only part of the equation.

Greed is also believing the lie that what you have is all there is. You wish others could have more pieces of the pie, but there's only so much to go around. It completely forgets that we can get more pies, bake more pies, and that we know the pie-maker.

Greed holds you back because it lies about the source of gain and its short-sightedness operates from a scarcity mindset, believing there's only so much to go around. Conversely, generosity realizes that we are stewards of God's abundant gifts, and it sees our close connection to the *Giver* of life as an endless wellspring to care for more. When we're generous, we most mirror the heart of our Good Father. In my experience, generosity is life-giving to the giver, and it's a difficult journey to master. However, the journey unlocks the future you most deeply desire.

GENEROSITY BEGINS WITH AN IMPORTANT PATTERN

In Luke 5, Jesus told Simon to let down his fishing nets. Simon obeyed, and he brought in the catch of his life. There's an important pattern in the story: obedience and blessing. When we obey, God blesses. Everyone wants God's will, but few people want to follow God's ways. But you'll never experience God's will unless you first commit to His ways. It's a divine pattern. It's how God works. Obedience and blessing.

Back in the Old Testament, God said this: "'If you walk in my statutes and observe my commandments and do them, then I will give you your rains in their season, and the land shall yield its increase, and the trees of the field shall yield their fruit'" (Leviticus 26:3-4). Do you see it? God says, "if you obey, I will bless." God is a good Father, and He *wants* to bless His children. God wants to bless you, your family, your relationships, and your calling. If you obey, God says, "I will bless."

Look again in the New Testament, and Jesus teaches us what to obey first. He's talking with people about their daily worries, and two thousand years later, this passage is enduringly relevant. Jesus told them, "'Therefore do not be anxious, saying, "What shall we eat?" or "What shall we drink?" or "What shall we wear?"'"

You may be reading this right now and you are all tied up in knots. You're anxious about today, and you're worried about tomorrow. You're apprehensive about what's ahead, and Jesus says you don't have to live that way. You can trade all your worries for one thing. Watch this: "'For the Gentiles seek after all these things, and your heavenly Father knows that you need them all. But seek first the kingdom of God and his righteousness, and all these things will be added to you'" (Matthew 6:32-33).

Jesus gets that we all have a destination in mind. We have desires and dreams. In fact, God made us with a destiny. He designed you with divine purpose. And Jesus says, "Look, I get it. I know there are a lot of cares in the world. But you can give me all of your worries, and I'll get you to your destination. To do this, you've got to focus on one thing. You must seek first." The Greek word for "seek" is *zeteo* (pronounced zay-tay-o), and it means "to seek in order to find." My kids love playing hide-and-seek, and we're ultra-competitive in our house. If you're the seeker, you're seeking in order to find. You're looking because you want to win. And this is how Jesus teaches us to seek His Kingdom, to seek in order to find what God has for us.

Where do you want to go? What's your dream? What's your destination? What impact do you want to have in the world? Where do you want the people in your life to end up? Jesus teaches that to get where we want to go, we must seek first the Kingdom of God, and God will get us to our greatest story. Obedience and blessing.

What are we seeking? We're going after the Kingdom of God. What does that mean? It all centers on Jesus. God sent Jesus to seek and save the lost. He's building a Kingdom of forgiven people—disciples who have been changed forever who go and make more disciples. There's a heavenly Kingdom coming, but it starts here on earth. To get to the destination God desires for us, we must seek first God's ways, God's desires, and God's will. It's not about us; it's about God. It's about God's children finding hope and forgiveness. Do you want a life filled with God's will and God's blessings, overflowing with divine purpose, making a difference for the Kingdom? Jesus says, "seek first," because what comes first matters most.

GOD ONLY RECEIVES THE FIRST . . .

God cannot be second. He's either first or nothing. Go back to the very beginning in Genesis 4. Notice the distinct postures with God that these two brothers had. Cain brought *an* offering. Abel brought the *firstborn*—the best he had to give. God rejected Cain's offering but accepted Abel's.

So, what do we do with the first? "'The first of the first fruits of your land you shall bring into the house of the Lord your God'" (Exodus 23:19 NKJV). For them it was the temple, today it's the local church. We—and I'm not excluded as a pastor—bring our first to God through the local church. We don't wait to see if there is enough and then give God our left-overs. Why? God only regards the first.

. . . BECAUSE GOD GAVE HIS FIRST

Why is God so focused on the first? God expects the first from us because He gave His first. Let me back up on this for a moment, going all the way to Exodus in the Old Testament, and then we'll come forward to Jesus. I think this could be a "lightbulb moment" for someone reading this as it was for me years ago when I first learned this important principle.[23]

> "After the Lord brings you into the land of the Canaanites and gives it to you, as he promised on oath to you and your ancestors, you are to give over to the Lord the first offspring of every womb. All the firstborn males of your livestock belong to the Lord." (Exodus 13:11-12 NIV)

God says, "the firstborn of your livestock, it comes back to me. Don't wait to sacrifice the runt, start with the first." They were to give the first and the best back to God. It continues, "Redeem with a lamb every firstborn donkey, but if you do not redeem it, break its neck. Redeem every firstborn among your sons" (Exodus 13:11-13).

Now, if that one went over your head, I promise you're not alone, but stay with me. There are two types of animals: clean and unclean. Animals like a lamb are clean. Animals like a donkey are unclean. The command here is this: If an unclean donkey is born, but you want to keep it, then you must redeem it with the life of a lamb.

Can you see what this foreshadows in the New Testament? As people born into this fallen and broken world, are we born clean or unclean? Spiritually speaking, we are unclean. We are born with a sinful nature. Was Jesus born clean or unclean? Jesus was conceived by the Holy Spirit. He was born clean, one hundred percent sinless, and one hundred percent perfect. And how is Jesus often described in the New Testament? The Lamb of God. Jesus is the *firstborn* Son of God; He's the Lamb of God who takes away the sins of the world. For those of us born unclean, Jesus is the clean Lamb of God who redeems our lives. You may not have memorized a lot of Scripture, but I'm guessing you may know this one:

"For God so loved the world, that he gave his only Son, that whoever believes in him should not perish but have eternal life" (John 3:16).

God did not wait on us. He gave His Son so that we could be made clean, whole, and new in Jesus. God gave His first, and what He asks of us He did *first*.

THE TITHE MUST BE FIRST

God only accepts the first. God gave His first. Now, we should ask ourselves, "What should be my response to these truths?" Our answer should be, "I must give my first and my best back to God." And the Bible teaches us that the tithe must be first.

A lot of people think a tithe is when you give a donation to a church. A tithe actually means a tenth, or ten percent. It isn't *any* donation; it's a tenth of how God has blessed you. It's the first ten percent of your income. This is why language is important. We shouldn't say that we're going to *take* an offering, or even that we *give* a tithe. In actuality, we *return* the tithe to God. It's all God's; we're merely the stewards of it. God is the giver and blesser. We return the tithe to God because God generously gives to us, and God deserves our first.

Now, let me stop for a moment. If the idea of giving the first ten percent of your income back to God is causing you to break out in hives, your body temperature to rise, and your heart rate to peak, take a deep breath. I've been there. I mean it. I was slow on learning this principle. Honestly, I held back our family for some time because my heart wasn't open to God on this principle. Katie got it. Katie wanted us to tithe, but I didn't get it. But once I got it, the peace and the blessing of God has been more evident in our lives. Again, there's a divine pattern. "If you obey, then I will bless." God wants to bless, but our obedience determines if we get to receive His blessings.

When we look back at the beginning of Scripture (Genesis 14 and 28), we learn that the tithe is a baseline response to God. Then, later, the Bible says in Leviticus, "Every tithe of the land, whether of the seed of the land or of the fruit of the trees, is the LORD's; it is holy to the LORD" (27:30). The tithe is holy to God. That means it is to be set apart or set aside to Him. That's why we say we return it to God. It not only comes from Him—it *is* His. The tithe, the first ten percent, is important to God.

I want you to take this in. Why? Because it has been life-changing for me, and I believe it will be for someone reading this. Look at another scripture with me.

> "Ever since the time of your ancestors you have turned away from my decrees and have not kept them. Return to me, and I will return to you," says the Lord Almighty. "But you ask, 'How are we to return?' Will a mere mortal rob God? Yet you rob me. But you ask,

'How are we robbing you?' In tithes and offerings. You are under a curse—your whole nation—because you are robbing me. Bring the whole tithe into the storehouse, that there may be food in my house. Test me in this," says the Lord Almighty, "and see if I will not throw open the floodgates of heaven and pour out so much blessing that there will not be room enough to store it." (Malachi 3:7-10 NIV)

Obedience and blessing. Israel was not following God's ways, so they were living outside of God's will. He said if they came back to His ways, they'd be back inside His will. The tithe is important, so God used strong language: "You're robbing me." The tithe is His, and we are to return it to Him. And if we do, God says, "I'll throw open the floodgates of blessing on your lives."

This principle is so core to our lives that it can be tough to digest. But I think that's part of the reason it's so important to God. Listen, God is not after your money. God doesn't need your income. God has never looked at any bank account with envy—not yours, not mine, not even Bill Gates'. God is after your heart. It's why Jesus said that where our treasure is, we'll find our heart also (See Matthew 6:21). And I love how God says, "Test Me!" God doesn't say that anywhere else in Scripture, so when He does, you better pay attention. God's saying, "I get it, you're not sure. So, test Me in it. Obey My ways and watch how I'll pour out My will and blessing in your life."

So, why not take God at His Word? Test Him! Seriously, try it for six months. I'm a living witness. From the day that we began returning the tithe back to God and to this day, God's blessings have not stopped. That doesn't mean there aren't challenges, or that everything is easy. But I do have great peace in our personal finances because I've learned that as I trust God with His ways, I can also trust that God will provide. And I've seen God bless us financially in ways that we could have never done for ourselves.

Years ago, I realized that I had neglected a tithe on the sale of a vehicle. I had purchased a car and then decided to sell it a couple months later. In the process, I made a $1,000 profit. Several weeks had passed when on a Sunday morning in church, I felt a gentle nudge from the Holy Spirit. It seemed like God was saying, "Don't forget to thank Me." Realizing my mistake, I returned to God ten percent of the profit. The next day, I had lunch with a friend, and he slid an envelope across the table, and he gave me these instructions:

"Chad, please open this after lunch, but don't thank me. God told me to do this and I'm just being obedient." The day before, I had tithed $100. Inside the envelope was $1,000. And can you guess my next move? That's right. I quickly tithed another $100.

Now, does God always financially bless me ten-fold each time that I tithe? Of course not. However, that day, God gave me a vivid picture in the natural world of what He is *always* doing in the spiritual world. When we follow God's ways, we are walking in His many blessings. And I've seen God repeat this story in various ways in my life and in so many others. Which also means that God's blessing is certainly not limited to our finances. To tie God's blessings to finances alone is really small thinking. But God will also bless our relationships, our families, our calling, our purpose, and our plans. God says, "If you will obey, I will bless." I see the blessing in the joy of our marriage, in the spiritual vitality of our kids, in the impact of ministry, and the countless opportunities we've had to share God's love with people across the world.

So often, we get hung up on the percentages. We think, *Ten percent? That's a lot of money!* But I want you to think about it differently. What did God say to Israel in the verse we just read? "You're living under a curse." What does that mean? You're living outside of God's blessing. Think of it like an umbrella. You're standing in the downpour, but if you'd come under God's authority, you'd come under His blessing. Ninety percent God's way is always better than one hundred percent your way. God will do for you what you can never do for yourself.

GOD ASKS MUCH OF THE FIRSTBORN

If you go back to the Old Testament book of Deuteronomy 21, God said that the firstborn son was to receive a double blessing from the father. It says that the firstborn had what they call in Hebrew a *mishpot*. That is often translated in English as a "right" or "privilege," but it can also be translated as a responsibility. So, the firstborn is given a double blessing as a responsibility because once the father was gone, the firstborn was to care for the family.

Fast-forward to the New Testament in Romans 8. Jesus was called the firstborn *among* many brothers and sisters. In other words, as followers of God's Son, we become firstborn children of God. Then, in Hebrews 12, the writer talks about the entire church as the firstborn of God. What does this mean? As people that have been redeemed by the Lamb of God, the firstborn of God's grace, we are given a double blessing. Why does God bless us? So that we can be a blessing. We have a right, or better said, a responsibility to take care of the world around us. God asks much of the firstborn.[24]

Imagine for a moment how generous the church could be if Christians took this responsibility seriously. Did you know that the resources needed to change the human condition are already inside the church? In America, somewhere between ten and twenty-five percent of members tithe. Think about that. According to God's Word, 75-90 percent are living under the curse, outside of God's blessing. But, if one hundred percent of American Christians began to trust God in this area of their life, it would generate $165 billion. Twenty-five billion dollars of that would eradicate global hunger and death from preventable diseases in five years. Twelve billion dollars would eliminate global illiteracy, again, in only five years. Fifteen billion dollars would solve water and sanitation issues globally. One billion dollars would fully fund all current overseas missions work. That would leave a measly $112 billion for sharing the gospel or addressing additional humanitarian needs.[25] God has provided the resources to eliminate significant human problems here on earth, but He can't get it out of the hands of the Church. The United States is a rich nation, but do we realize that we are blessed so that we can be a blessing? If we simply trusted God with the first ten percent, God could change the world through our generosity.

MAKE ME GENEROUS

So, let me go back to my first question: Where do you want to go? Are your actions and your priorities taking you there? Jesus says to seek first His Kingdom, and He'll take care of the rest. God only accepts the first. God gave His first. We return to God the tithe first. And we accept the responsibility of the firstborn. We are blessed to be a blessing.

As children immeasurably blessed by God, we must stand in awe of God's great kindness and grace to us. Our response should be that we want our lives to count. We must stand with our hands raised to God in submission and passion, saying, "God, we desire to live on mission, full of purpose and passion!"

If your priorities have been misaligned, come back to the words of Jesus, and seek first the Kingdom. Put Jesus at the forefront, declaring that nothing else is as important as Him. Put God first and be astonished at the thought that God gave *you* His firstborn Son! Consider it a privilege to give back to God your first and your best. Ask God to make the tithe the starting point. Let it be a new place of trust for you today. I personally know how powerful it is to trust God with the tithe. When you get the order right, it begins to birth generosity in your heart and opens your life to the fullness that God desires for you. Then, you'll take up the baton of the firstborn and accept your responsibility to join God in bringing His Kingdom here on earth. Maybe even whisper this prayer: "God, use my life, my gifts, and my talents to echo Your love. Oh God, make me generous."

QUESTIONS *for* TRANSFORMATION

1. What are some ways that a mindset of entitlement has held you back?

2. Who are some people that deserve your gratitude?

3. How could some challenging circumstances in your life transform if you chose to find gratitude within them?

4. How will you craft a heart posture of gratitude in your daily life?

5. Why is generosity the on-ramp to a life of purpose and impact?

6. How have you seen God's blessings in your life as you walk in obedience to God's ways?

7. What is your next step in growing in the principle of generosity?

"For the great doesn't happen through impulse alone and is a succession of little things that are brought together."

—VINCENT VAN GOGH[26]

CHAPTER 11

FOCUS ON "WHO" OVER "DO"

Have you ever had a moment sneak up on you? When I was a young youth pastor, I had one of those moments when the matter seemed small but its gravity was far more than meets the eye.

Our church had a thriving student ministry comprised of a student wing with offices, classrooms, and a gymnasium, complete with a stage and storage. Only in retrospect do I fully grasp the blessings encompassed in those amazing spaces. For a season, there were two of us young guys at the helm of this ministry. Our cumulative ages were still less than that of a young middle-aged man, and yet we were given leadership far beyond our years, part of which was the oversight of these facilities. Thankfully, we had a tremendous team of custodians and a head custodian that cared not only about our church and its ministries, but he also wasn't afraid of training up young men. Richard kept the entire church in immaculate condition, and he expected us to do the same. Our gymnasium was mostly used by the student ministry but not solely. It was a multi-purpose space, and he helped us keep it hospitable for all ministries and guests.

Our creative and innovative student ministry was always busy with big programming from professional bands to music competitions, to office chair jousting, to human car pulls, all with massive gatherings involving hundreds of students. So, when Richard asked me and the other student pastor to be sure to pick up a handful of cords and mics that were left on the stage, it wasn't a big deal to either of us. "Sure, no problem," we said.

In truth, I think we were both slightly frustrated that our efforts to return the space back to zero wasn't appreciated. Instead, what was recognized was what remained, which we thought was relatively small and insignificant.

"Hey guys, remember, we have an event in the gym this evening," Richard reminded us again. "Please remove the equipment left on the stage."

"Yep, no worries," we responded. Except we got busy, forgot, and never did what was asked of us, nor what we said we would do.

The next day, Richard called us to account. In fact, he called me to the carpet. I don't know if I was the bigger offender or if I was the first one he ran into. Either way, I got the lesson.

"Chad, do you remember those cords and mics that I asked you to pick up? While preparing the gymnasium for an event last night, I had to stop and clean up your mess, too. I asked you to do it. You told me you would do it. This is a matter of integrity, and it doesn't make you look like a leader."

Now, I think it's necessary to state that Richard was an incredibly kind person. Don't picture an old curmudgeon. He was neither old nor crusty. In this moment, he needed to teach me a lesson, and he did.

Richard was one hundred percent right. It *was* a matter of integrity. And while I had downplayed it as a small thing and no big deal, small things make a big difference. As a growing leader, it's more important to focus on *who you are becoming* than it is on what you do. Expanding your character is less about the big things we do and more about the small choices about who we want to become. At his core, Richard was resounding with the wise man Solomon, who said, "A rebuke goes deeper into a man of understanding than a hundred blows into a fool." (Proverbs 17:10)

If gratitude and generosity are magnetic to God, then qualities like integrity and wholeness are magnetic to the people in our lives. Think about it with the people in your life right now. You have those that you can count on to do what they said. They don't over-promise and under-deliver. If anything, they over-deliver. Conversely, you know people who seldom do all that they said they would do. Now, take some stock of how you are perceived. Do an honest gut check. Do you deliver, or are you regularly coming up short of what you said? Listen—you can't get better until you're first willing to get real.

This is why Paul directed the Colossians accordingly: "Whatever you do, work at it with all your heart, as working for the Lord, not for human masters . . . It is the Lord Christ you are serving" (Colossians 3:23-24 NIV). *How* you lead is important because it reflects who you are becoming. Your actions will always speak louder than your words, especially when your actions don't align with your words. Alignment is integrity, and as we'll discover in this chapter, it gives birth to a whole heart. These qualities are not merely helpful tools; they are byproducts of a heart fixed on becoming better rather than a hurried soul set on simply accomplishing more.

INTEGRITY

Read this passage with me:

> The next day as they were leaving Bethany, Jesus was hungry. Seeing in the distance a fig tree in leaf, he went to find out if it had any fruit. When he reached it, he found nothing but leaves because it was not the season for figs. Then he said to the tree, "May no one ever eat fruit from you again." And his disciples heard him say it.

151

On reaching Jerusalem, Jesus entered the temple courts and began driving out those who were buying and selling there. He overturned the tables of the money changers and the benches of those selling doves and would not allow anyone to carry merchandise through the temple courts. And as he taught them, he said, "Is it not written: 'My house will be called a house of prayer for all nations'? But you have made it 'a den of robbers.'"

The chief priests and the teachers of the law heard this and began looking for a way to kill him, for they feared him, because the whole crowd was amazed at his teaching.

When evening came, Jesus and his disciples went out of the city.

In the morning, as they went along, they saw the fig tree withered from the roots. Peter remembered and said to Jesus, "Rabbi, look! The fig tree you cursed has withered!"

"Have faith in God," Jesus answered. "Truly I tell you, if anyone says to this mountain, 'Go, throw yourself into the sea,' and does not doubt in their heart but believes that what they say will happen, it will be done for them. Therefore I tell you, whatever you ask for in prayer, believe that you have received it, and it will be yours. And when you stand praying, if you hold anything against anyone, forgive them, so that your Father in heaven may forgive you your sins." (Mark 11:12-25 NIV)

Without context, this is perhaps one of the strangest stories in the gospels. Why is Jesus angry with a tree, and why does He waste his time cursing it? Besides, if it wasn't the season for figs, what was Jesus expecting to find? Thankfully for us, Mark is a skilled writer, and he gives us clues as to what's going on with Jesus. First, the fig tree was "in leaf," which meant that it gave the appearance of being full of fruit. While it wasn't the season for figs, the tree's exterior held the promise for harvest. Jesus then moved in closer to inspect it, pulled aside the leaves, and found nothing. The tree lacked integrity.

Next, Jesus entered the city of Jerusalem, and He saw the temple. From a distance, it gave the impression of the house of God where people could seek God's presence and receive God's love. However, upon closer inspection, Jesus found it lacking. Rather than a refuge for prayer, it had become a town square, complete with buying and selling. Instead of a place of grace and mercy, the money changers and the merchants took advantage of the people. Those who would travel a great distance could not bring their animal sacrifice with them, so they would have to buy at the temple. Since they had traveled a long way, they first had to exchange their money to the local currency. The money changers would price gouge the traveler for a simple reason: They could.

Unfortunately, even today, greedy merchants take advantage of desperate people. We saw it during the COVID-19 crisis, when toilet paper was scarce and shops began to charge extravagant prices. Why? Because they could.

After they were taken for a ride by the money changers, the travelers—often quite poor—would then do business with those selling the animals. During religious festivals, prices could be inflated as much as twenty times the normal amount. For instance, if toilet paper normally costs seven dollars, in this context, it would cost $140.

This is what Jesus walked into. People traveled from distant lands to faithfully follow God. Then, the money changers and animal sellers extorted them, and most were desperately poor. They may have lost months of wages just to pray to God inside the temple. Now, you've got to understand all of that to understand what Jesus did next. He overturned the tables and drove out those doing business. When Jesus saw the fig tree, it lacked integrity. When Jesus entered the temple, it broke His heart. Jesus became righteously angry. He saw greed and hypocrisy, abuse of people, and misuse of His Father's house. So, Jesus did something you don't see very often in the gospel stories; He got angry, and He got aggressive. He was angry on behalf of those who were mistreated. The temple gave the appearance of a place where people could experience God's grace and mercy. It lacked integrity. Rather than being a house of prayer, it had become a "den of robbers."

Finally, the story concludes with a teaching from Jesus that at first glance appears to have little to do with what just took place. In reality, it gets to the heart of what Jesus is revealing to His followers. They saw the withered fig tree and their jaws hit the floor. "Jesus," they proclaimed, "you just cursed this tree yesterday and today it's dead!"

Jesus responded, "Oh, fellas. If you only knew. You see, I'm going to give you this kind of authority too. If you have faith, you can move mountains!" And then Jesus came in with an important disclaimer, "But, you cannot pray with a sincere heart while also withholding forgiveness for another."

And with this, Jesus tidily wrapped up the message of the past twenty-four hours. "Jerusalem was supposed to be a place where people from all over the world could come to pray and experience the presence of my Father. However, it lacks integrity. In time, I'm going to send you to the corners of the world. You will be my temples, extending the presence of God across the globe. You must have integrity. You must represent me. I'm the same on the outside as on the inside. You cannot pray and at the same time withhold forgiveness. You must extend grace and be an extension of my love." When our outside life matches our interior growth, integrity is being formed. And how we cultivate the interior growth is incredibly important.

EMPTY PURSUITS

When Katie and I were moving to L.A., I had a visualization of what it looked like to live the good life as a SoCal resident. I had visions of enjoying the beach, life in the city, and magical trips to Disneyland with our baby girl (soon to be *girls*). In particular, I wanted us to shine like celebrities in the sun along L.A.'s city beaches. To be clear, I have never spotted a single celebrity at the beach. Those sightings happened at more mundane locations like Ikea and the Apple store. Though, we twice ran into my all-time favorite basketball player, Kobe Bryant, at Disneyland. On one occasion, I'm pretty sure he gave Ava the flu. She sat in his seat at the caboose after he departed the Casey Junior train ride. Later that day, she became sick, and he dropped out of that night's lineup due to flu-like symptoms. I'm just saying . . .

In my L.A. vision, we would cruise on "The Strand" along Manhattan Beach, a paved running, biking, and roller-blading path that stretched down to Hermondo and Redondo Beaches. To a lifetime Midwesterner, this was really living. We bought nice bikes at a cycle shop in Pasadena, along with a tow-rack for the car, a storage rack for our apartment, and a sweet seat for Ava to ride on my bike. I could envision it: There I was, shades on, rolling next to my beautiful bride with my baby girl in tow (and of course, she was also wearing shades). In the words of Beck, this was "where it's at!"

Of course, reality is different, and it requires more sweat and probably more tears than imagined in the dream. In our first outing, after fighting L.A. traffic to get to the beach with a cranky toddler, it then took us thirty minutes just to find a spot to park in the city of Manhattan Beach. Then, perched above the town, we trekked at least a half-mile down to the beach, arms full of beach gear. Wanting to enjoy some "beach time" before our maiden voyage, I sat the whole time wondering if someone was stealing our bikes displayed gloriously on the back of our Nissan Xterra. When I couldn't take it anymore, we trekked back up to the car, unhooked the bikes, and proceeded back down to the Strand, dodging traffic and balancing a toddler on the back of my bike. Once we finally made it, my nerves were shot, my body was tired, and the dream felt more like a nightmare.

Determined not to give up on my idea of L.A. living, I decided that our next grand outing would be riding around the canyon at the Rose Bowl. Just minutes down the road from our apartment, this made a lot of sense.

Parking was plentiful and it's beautiful—what could go wrong? As we took off, Katie and I realized that each of our bikes had a flat tire. I lost my marbles. I told Katie that we were going home, taking photos of every item, and selling them on Craigslist (Anybody remember Craigslist?). I wasn't kidding. I was done with this ridiculous fantasy. Thankfully, Katie helped me calm down and be reasonable, and we still have the bikes to this day.

Why was I so frustrated? The bikes and the locations were supposed to make me *feel* better about my life, but they left me feeling empty. In truth, the emptiness was already there. The bikes merely highlighted the truth that soul problems can't be fixed with things we see. Our hearts are longing for wholeness, but since true wholeness is spiritual, only spiritual things can quench our thirst.

Most of us have experienced our "bikes on the Strand" pursuits, where something external was supposed to fix an internal problem. Rather than filling us up, these hollow quests leave us stranded and empty. You chased after something, you got it, and it was supposed to make you feel better. Except it didn't. *I've just got to get on vacation*, you tell yourself. Sitting at the beach, you ask yourself, *Now what?* Or, *Well, I just need to buy that new truck,* but then the loan payments begin and the new car smell fades. *When I get that job, when my income reaches this level, then the problems will fade,* you convince yourself. But the problems don't fade away because you're trying to address the fruit, but there's a root problem.

During the COVID-19 pandemic, this became reality for many people. Crisis accelerates everything. Things that would have proven hollow over time were suddenly revealed for what they were. The things that so many leaned on were taken away overnight, and they proved to be shaky wooden crutches rather than firm foundations.

Have you ever tried to guard your fall and ended up causing more harm than just allowing yourself to fall? Perhaps you tried to stay upright and ended up twisting a knee. Or you grasped for help and held on to something sharp or put your elbow through a wall. In much the same way, as people fall in crises, they cling to bikes on the Strand, which only exacerbates and accelerates a sense of emptiness. As people grew sad, lonely, angry, and confused, RV, boat, and pool sales skyrocketed during the pandemic. So did alcohol sales and pornographic site visits. Depression soared. Hope plummeted.

Outside of a global crisis, you've heard or perhaps even said, "I just need some downtime." So, you buy some new clothes, read a book, play some golf, or go fishing. The achievers among us get the promotion, make the sale, nail the grade, or run a marathon. Others seek after connections like friendships or romance, but in needing something from the relationship, they end up draining it. "Just get me to the weekend," the tired soul proclaims. Pursuing comforts isn't inherently wrong, but they become bikes on the Strand if they take the place of true and lasting wholeness. When we try to satisfy our soul's thirst for the eternal with the temporal, we're always left feeling empty.

GIFTS OR THE GIVER?

Consider God's admonition to the people of Israel through the prophet Jeremiah: "'But my people have exchanged their glorious God for worthless idols'" (Jeremiah 2:11 NIV).

It seems ridiculous, doesn't it? How could God's people leave their Creator, Promise Maker, and Miracle Worker? And yet, they did. They left the Most High God for man-made, inanimate objects that have never done and could never do anything for them. And yet, isn't that precisely what we do when we expect things of earth to satisfy soul longings? *When I get that car,* we think. *Well, when I get that financial bonus; when I can finally take that vacation;* or *when I make that grade and get the college entrance letter of my dreams,* we believe, *then I'll finally be happy and my problems will subside.* Except they don't. These are man-made, inanimate objects that never have and never can do anything for us.

God continues, "'Be appalled at this, you heavens, and shudder with great horror,'" (v. 12). Think about what God was asking of the skies. He wanted them to be appalled at what's happening on earth, and therefore to shudder and recoil from it. If the skies shudder from us, what happens? The rain stops, and we're toast. The Hebrew word that God used here is *harab* (pronounced khaw-rab), and it means "to be dried up." God was saying that if we chose earthly objects over a faith-filled relationship with him, our souls would dry up.

Of course, the people of God think that they have found a way around the problem, and yet God declared they had created an even bigger mess. "'My people have committed two sins: They have forsaken me, the spring of living water, and have dug their own cisterns, broken cisterns that cannot hold water'" (v. 13). They have forsaken God, the spring of living water, which dried up their souls. Then, they attempted to dig cisterns in order to quench their thirst. God is saying, "These are bogus basins, they cannot hold living water, only a soul can do that." We do this, too. We look to physical gratification, like hobbies and experiences, or food and substances. If we can pursue prestige, we wrongly believe, this will contain the life we're thirsty for. We think that the more we achieve, the less we'll feel the emptiness. "Once I achieve success through my career, the more possessions I acquire, the more I appear to have it all together, this will fill the void." Or we run after relationships, hoping that they'll complete us. In the end, rather than bringing something to the relationships, we end up draining them, because we're empty. Ideologies will do the trick, we think. "I'll have the right beliefs, an immense amount of knowledge, or the pride of politics." In the end, these are all vacuous vessels that pour out, rather than filling up.

There isn't inherent evil in most of these pursuits. The problem comes when the pursuits take precedence over the Provider, the gifts over the Giver. Augustine nailed it: "Thou has made us for Thyself, and our hearts are restless till they find rest in Thee."[27] They are all signs pointing to the Creator, declaring His goodness and provision. But when we seek them over Him, the skies hold back the rain and our souls become dry.

DRY BONES, HEAR THE WORD OF THE LORD

"Can these bones live?" This audacious question is made even more remarkable by the One asking it. God is talking to Ezekiel while overlooking a valley of dry bones. The prophet wisely responds, "'Lord God, only you know'" (Ezekiel 37:3). The nation of Israel was grumbling to God because of their barren conditions. Yet, their empty pursuits led them to resemble the valley of dead and dry bones.

Perhaps you've asked this question before in reference to your own life. Maybe you're asking that question today. Quite often, we'll also grumble to God when the thing we pursued leaves us feeling empty. But we must see the things of earth for what they are: mirages in the desert. Pursue them if you must, but be ready for a mouth full of sand and a grasping after the wind.

So, what do you do when your soul is thirsty?

"Dry bones," God declares, "hear the word of the Lord." It's not surprising that God's answer to our dry souls is his Word. The writer of Hebrews proclaims that "the word of God is alive and active" (4:12 NIV). What can cause a dried-up soul to live again but that which is alive and active?

God's words animate and elevate. Jesus *is* the Word that spoke creation into being. And He is the Word that speaks our dry bones back to life. When the dry bones heard the Word of the Lord, they came back together. You and I must be close enough to God to hear His words, and we must obey His Word in order to receive His living water.

When we realize that the things of earth have replaced God Himself, James tells us to wash our hands and purify our hearts: "Humble yourselves before the Lord, and he will lift you up in honor" (4:10 NLT).

John reminds us that the things of earth offer only "a craving for physical pleasure, a craving for everything we see" (1 John 2:16 NLT). In essence, what appears to satisfy only intensifies the hunger and longing. "But anyone who does what pleases God will live forever" (v. 17).

In Haggai, God said when our priorities are misaligned, "You eat but are not satisfied. You drink but are still thirsty" (Haggai 1:6 NLT). When Jesus was hungry and tempted by the devil to turn stones to bread, He responded, "'Man shall not live by bread alone, but by every word that comes from the mouth of God'" (Matthew 4:4). Jesus knew that if it wasn't in His Father's will, that the bread would be like gravel in his mouth. It was His knowledge of God's Word that sustained Him. Having first-hand experience with the tempter, Jesus declares, "'The thief comes only to steal and kill and destroy. I came that they may have life and have it abundantly'" (John 10:10). When your soul is dry, start with the Word that gives life; obey what He speaks.

AND YOU SHALL LIVE

Once Ezekiel prophesied to the dry bones, he heard a rattling as the bones came back together. However, they still needed life. So, God said, "'I will cause breath to enter you'" (Ezekiel 37:5). As God spoke to Israel's future hope and purpose, God continued, "'I will put my Spirit within you, and you shall live'" (Ezekiel 37:14). In the Old Testament, God's Spirit was called *ruach* (pronounced roo-akh), and God said that the people would find life when His breath, His *ruach*, was within them.

In the New Testament, Jesus spoke of the Holy Spirit (*pneuma*, pronounced noo-mah) coming upon us (Acts 1:8), and it's then that we receive power to witness to God's love and life. Later on, the Apostle Paul tells us that when we walk in the *pneuma*, we "will not gratify the desires of the flesh" (Galatians 5:16).

As we hear the Word of the Lord, we learn that God's breath can come inside of us and give us spiritual life and power. God did not design us to (nor does God expect us to) come up with life, wisdom, and strength on our own. Rather, we're taught to live from the Spirit's dwelling within us. As we spend time in God's Word, we stay close enough to get God's breath on us and in us. As we live out God's Word, the Spirit empowers us. As we walk in obedience, God's favor and grace go with us, "'For the eyes of the Lord range throughout the earth to strengthen those whose hearts are fully committed to him'" (2 Chronicles 16:9 NIV).

When we discover that emptiness has made its home in our hearts, it's time to resurrect dry bones. We've pursued the things of earth instead of their Creator. We've left God for worthless idols. In turn, we reap the harvest of a dried-up soul from the seeds we've sown. If we seek out broken cisterns, we're left with shuddered skies and "pockets filled with holes" (Haggai 1:6 NLT)!

So, we recognize our ways, we return to God in humility, and He lifts us up. We are meant to saturate ourselves with God's Word and invite His Spirit to revive us. Integrity aligns my outer world with my inner growth, while hollow pursuits fall away and make room for a whole heart. When our focus shifts to who we're becoming over merely accomplishing more things, dry bones and barren cisterns give way to a flourishing life. As we live from gratitude, the Living Water takes over, and we become generative wellsprings for those around us.

QUESTIONS for TRANSFORMATION

1. Like the barren fig tree, in what ways can people give the appearance of fruitfulness while their lives actually lack integrity?

2. How does integrity impact the effectiveness of your leadership?

3. In what ways have you pursued the things of earth when your soul actually craved the things of God?

4. If your life feels like dry bones, how will you pursue God and envelope your life with the Word of the Lord?

ATTRIBUTE 5
MADE to SOAR

Kill Comparison, Pummel Procrastination

"I have fought the good fight, I have finished the race, I have kept the faith."

—2 Timothy 4:7

"We won't be distracted by comparison if we're captivated with purpose."

—BOB GOFF[28]

CHAPTER 12

RUN YOUR RACE

In January of 2011, I wanted to try my hand at a new mode of transportation. We lived close to Duke University's campus, and I was participating in advanced graduate studies. In Durham, and especially close to campus, it was extremely common for people to commute on two wheels. *Lots of people do it,* I reasoned. *How hard can it be?*

Now, do you remember the bike I thought was going to produce my dreams of the good life in L.A.? That bike is making it into another story.

On this day, it was particularly cold, so I wore my winter jacket and stocking cap, tossed on my backpack, and I was off. Now, if you've ever been to Durham, it has far more hills than you might realize. Duke's campus is especially hilly. By the time I made it to campus, I had removed my jacket and cap, my backpack was dangling from my bike, and I had fully saturated my shirt from sweating so profusely. After I locked my bike to a rack, I sat outside for the next thirty minutes, hoping to cool down and dry off. Did I mention it was January? I was late to class and had to sit away from the other students because I was afraid that I'd give off the "I've just been to the gym" smell.

My new mode of transportation to Duke's campus lasted one day. *One day.* If it isn't apparent by now, biking is not for me. It may be a preferred method for commuting in Durham, on L.A. beaches, and for millions of others across the world, but evidently, I'm not meant for it. I actually love to run. Funny enough, I regularly ran the same route that I biked that day. I ran in the sweltering heat of North Carolina summers and the icy mornings in the winter, and I loved every minute. On my runs, I'd pray, think, dream, and at times, hear God's still, small voice.

What's my point? I literally had to run my own race, and it has regularly been my source of joy and renewal. Yours might be biking, walking, swimming, or using a mobility aid.

As we pursue our God-given story, we've got to run *our* race.

COMPARISON IS A PUNK

When you set out to write your story, you'll be tempted to look all around you. And while it's fine and even advisable to learn from others, their lives are not yours. You don't have their context, their struggles, their calling, or their unique constitution. You are made with your own constellation of quirks, joys, fears, and triumphs. I like how Bob Goff summarizes it: "Comparison is a punk." Enough said.[29] Comparison will kill momentum, or it will simply leave you at the starting blocks, afraid to even begin. Comparison can make you feel so small, it's laden with lies, and it has no place in living your greatest story and pursuing God's path for your life.

Rather than comparison, we need to focus on obedience to the story God's created us to live. Throughout this book, you hear the whispers of God pointing you in a direction. While you'll continue to narrow in on God's call, necessarily take some detours, and even plan new routes, you've got to run *your* race. No one else can do it for you, and you can't live someone else's life; only yours. Comparison is short sighted, focusing on the right here and right now. You'll think that someone else is ahead of you with a better life, a better job, a better car, with better vacations. Obedience has a higher perspective, where you can see the whole journey. Rather than limiting your sights on the here and now, you realize that today is not the whole story. You have no idea how God will shower favor on your obedience.

Comparison puts you at odds with the people around you. Rather than cheering them on, they become obstacles to get over and get around. Yet, you've already chosen to fight *for* them, not *against* them. Obedience remembers that elevating the people around you is the goal—not beating them to the finish line. Comparison derails you from God's plan. It's the equivalent of texting while driving on a mountain road. You can't get where you're going when you take your eyes off of your path. If you do, be ready for the cliff that's coming. Wise Solomon says that "A heart at peace gives life to the body, but envy rots the bones" (Proverbs 14:30 NIV).

Comparison makes you feel like you've got to catch up in some imaginary race, but obedience will be your guide to help you arrive right on time. You won't be wondering if you've missed out, or if someone else has it better. You'll be focused on living your story, knowing that God will fulfill his purpose for your life.

The writer of Hebrews understood this: ". . . let us lay aside every weight, and the sin which so easily ensnares us, and let us run with endurance the race that is set before us" (Hebrews 12:1 NKJV). Comparison is sin because it ensnares and entangles, and it takes our eyes off of God's best for our lives. Instead of looking to the sides, we find life when we are "looking unto Jesus, the author and finisher of our faith, who for the joy that was set before Him endured the cross, despising the shame, and has sat down at the right hand of the throne of God" (v. 2). Jesus could have easily chosen a different path. He could have chosen a simpler path, but obedience compelled Him to live His greatest story. In obedience He chose the cross, and in obedience He set us free. In time, He sat down at the right hand of God. Living a comparison life would have been easier at the time, but it would have had less impact, and in the end, less glory.

COMPARISON SETTLES FOR LESS

Throughout the story of God's people, the Israelites, there is a continual disobedience, and it often stems from comparison. As they looked around at the other nations, instead of seeing that they were the chosen people of God, they often became envious. From the benefit of hindsight, this is crazy. While they were willing to settle for less, God wanted to make them the pinnacle nation. One of my favorite Old Testament verses spells this out. In Isaiah 49, God told Israel how He wanted to bring them back to the promise that He had for them. But, God said bringing them back was only part of the plan. "'It is too light a thing that you should be my servant to raise up the tribes of Jacob and to bring back the preserved of Israel; I will make you as a light for the nations, that my salvation may reach to the end of the earth'" (Isaiah 49:6). Bringing back the preserved of Israel was no problem. But that was just the beginning.

God wanted Israel to be the light for the nations, the city on a hill, whom all the nations of the world would look upon and say, "These people are favored by God because they follow Him in obedience." In this, the love of God could echo across the globe. In time, God would fulfill this promise through Jesus, the Son of God, born an Israelite. And yet, the people of God were willing to forfeit their legacy in order to look like other nations.

As Israel was learning to follow God, they were guided by judges. They don't have an earthly king because as God's people, He was their King. But as the prophet Samuel was guiding them, they began to ask for an earthly king. Samuel was deeply saddened, so God told him, "'They have not rejected you, but they have rejected me from being king over them'" (1 Samuel 8:7). Samuel attempted to discourage the people, warning them that they didn't know what they were asking and that earthly kings would lead them away from following God and lead their children into battles. "But the people refused to obey the voice of Samuel. And they said, 'No! But there shall be a king over us, that we also may be like all the nations, and that our king may judge us and go out before us and fight our battles'" (1 Samuel 8:19-20). There's only one problem: They were never supposed to be like other nations. They were supposed to be *the light* to the other nations. They didn't need to have an earthly king fight their battles; God already promised to fight their battles (Deuteronomy 1:30; 3:22; 20:4).

As followers of Jesus, we find many parallels with the first people of God. We aren't supposed to look around and try to be like the world. Jesus said, "'You are the light of the world'" (Matthew 5:14). The more we try to look like someone else, the less we're getting it right. The more distinct we are, the closer we are to God's unique plan for our lives.

Growing up in a Jewish family, the Apostle Peter would have understood this. His ancestors lost their distinctness in favor of looking like the world. But, as a follower of Jesus, a new people would emerge. Peter tells us, ". . . you are a chosen generation, a royal priesthood, a holy nation, His own special people, that you may proclaim the praises of Him who called you out of darkness into His marvelous light; who once were not a people but are now the people of God . . ." (1 Peter 2:9-10 NKJV).

THE HIGH COST OF COMPARISON

I wish I could say that pastors were above comparison, but we're human too. In fact, early in my ministry, I came face-to-face with the high cost of comparison.

It wasn't the first time I had delivered a message, but it was the first time at this particular church. I greatly admired the lead pastor and the youth pastor, and I worked really hard to speak with their level of wisdom and winsomeness.

The opportunity came for me to speak to the student ministry, and I was beyond excited and extremely nervous. I studied, prayed, made notes, and I thought I was ready. I stepped in front of the group, ready to "wow" them. No words came out. I looked at my notes, and they made zero sense. I looked at the youth pastor whom I deeply admired standing in the back. He motioned with his hands that I should pray.

In hindsight, I think he was suggesting that I should pray, collect myself, and begin. Instead, I briefly prayed, said, "amen," and quickly exited stage right. My whole message lasted forty-five seconds at most. Thankfully, they didn't give up on me, and many more chances would emerge. My desire to speak like my pastors led to a complete inability to speak at all. And while the high cost of comparison rarely leads to such immediate humiliation, in truth, its effects are often far more harmful than my embarrassment that day.

I also wish that I could say that I've graduated from the temptation to compare in ministry. Two decades later, the desire to level up to an imaginary standard still lurks. In fact, social media has only exacerbated the problem for us all. As a church planter, I once had a nationally influential leader tell me that in his experience, all church planters are lying on social media. I think he was trying to encourage me, but I was deeply discouraged from the conversation. Church planting is already extremely difficult without the added external pressures that we were heaping on one another. While I was laboring nonstop to care for my family, deliver great messages, lead our team with excellence, and reach out to our community, I often lived with a nagging voice that more was needed.

In the Old Testament, God was trying to set apart Israel as His own nation. They were to be distinct, a nation pointing the rest of the world to a good and holy God. Instead, they desired to be like everyone else, which was far less than God's best.

The story that God is writing in your life won't look like those around you. God wants to write an original manuscript that is you. Learn from others and grow, but don't be limited by what others have done or by what you see around you. Moreover, don't *partially* do what God asks you to do; go all-in. Let go of bad attitudes and destructive habits. Forgive when you're hurt by others, be generous, serve others, and live boldly the life God is unfolding in you.

DO YOU FEEL OVERLOOKED?

For generations Israel fumbled around, comparing themselves to the nations around them, and this produced disobedience to God. King Saul was the personification of their generational missteps. The future king, David, would foreshadow the coming Christ. Saul represented Israel's desire to be like other nations. David prefigured the coming Christ, the light to the nations, and the salvation of the world.

If that wasn't enough, can I share some additional good news with you? While David would in time become Israel's great king and point to the Savior King, no one saw it coming. If you've been overlooked, passed up, and underappreciated, you're in good company with David. No one, not even his own father, saw greatness in him. Samuel arrived in Bethlehem to anoint a king among Jesse's sons. He paraded seven of his sons before Samuel asked, "Are all your sons here?" Only then did Jesse confess, "'There remains yet the youngest, but behold, he is keeping the sheep'" (1 Samuel 16:11). Beyond wanting to inconvenience Samuel, Jesse was insinuating that they think so little of David, they had given him the important job of watching sheep eat.

FAITHFULNESS IS THE KEY TO YOUR DESTINY

I not only love David because he was an underdog but because of what he was doing when Samuel showed up in town. David wasn't at a training camp for future kings. He wasn't sitting in a palace, nor was he lax on his work. He was doing precisely what his father tasked him to do: keeping the sheep.

Later we learn that while the work of a shepherd may seem mundane, David was quite the action hero. He would later take down lions and bears to protect the sheep. Being a shepherd wasn't something he did; it was who he was. Please do not miss this because it is critical: David was faithful right where he was. He wasn't putting out his resume and telling the other herdsman that his dad underappreciated his talents. He wasn't cutting corners. When David got his big break, he was being faithful. Let me double down on that. When David got his big break, it was *because* he was being faithful. He was obedient to his earthly father, and his heavenly Father took notice. David reminds us that faithfulness is the key that unlocks our destiny.

David wasn't behind or ahead; he was right on time. This is underscored in the next chapter. Israel was at battle with the Philistines, who put forth their best fighter and a proposition: "If you can beat our giant, we'll all be your slaves" (1 Samuel 17:8-9, paraphrased). During the siege, Jesse sent David with food for his oldest brothers, who were all at the Israelite camp. On this fateful trip, I love what the scriptures record for us: "So David rose early in the morning, left the sheep with a keeper, and took the things and went as Jesse had commanded him" (1 Samuel 17:20).

He was not only faithful to his father's new commands; he was faithful to the responsibility his father had given him in the past. Before setting out, he made sure the sheep were cared for; he was, after all, the forerunner of the Good Shepherd.

YOUR ARMOR IS ENOUGH

When David arrived at the camp, he learned of the proposition and that no one, not even his own brothers, would step forward to fight the Philistine champion. David could not believe that they all trusted God so little that they would allow one man to defy them. He approached the rejected king, Saul, and spoke with holy confidence,

> "Your servant has killed both lion and bear; and this uncircumcised Philistine will be like one of them, seeing he has defied the armies of the living God." He continued, "The LORD, who delivered me from the paw of the lion and from the paw of the bear, He will deliver me from the hand of this Philistine" (1 Samuel 17:36-37 NKJV).

The reigning king had fumbled his leadership, led the nation in disobedience, and was afraid to step forward and fight. The future king was assured that the Lord reigned and was ready for the fight.

While Saul was concerned to let a youth fight the battle, he was also out of options. It should be of no surprise to us that Saul tried to outfit David with his own royal armor. After all, Saul was appointed because Israel wanted to pretend to be other nations. Now, he wanted David to pretend to be a mature and mighty warrior; he wasn't, at least not yet. He was a shepherd boy.

With integrity of heart and trust in God, David stepped forth clothed only as himself. There was no comparison, no envy. David would approach the giant the only way he knew how: "Then he took his staff in his hand; and he chose five smooth stones from the brook, and put them in his shepherd's bag, in a pouch which he had, and his sling was in his hand. And he drew near to the Philistine" (1 Samuel 17:40). The shepherd was ready to protect the sheep of Israel.

For so long, David and Goliath have been known as the classic underdog tale. Yet, I love how Malcolm Gladwell reframes the story—where David is the odds-on favorite. "Slinging," Gladwell notes, "took an extraordinary amount of skill and practice. But in experienced hands, the sling was a devastating weapon."[30] Gladwell continues, "Goliath had as much chance against David as any Bronze Age warrior with a sword would have had against an [opponent] armed with a .45 automatic pistol."[31] In short, Goliath brought a big piece of metal to a gun fight. And while I greatly appreciate this understanding of the story, the true advantage wasn't David's skill; it was his faith in God and his trust that God was with him just as he was.

> Then David said to the Philistine, "You come to me with a sword, with a spear, and with a javelin. But I come to you in the name of the LORD of hosts, the God of the armies of Israel, whom you have defied. This day the LORD will deliver you into my hand, and I will strike you and take your head from you. And this day I will give the carcasses of the camp of the Philistines to the birds of the air and the wild beasts of the earth, that all the earth may know that there is a God in Israel. Then all this assembly shall know that the LORD does not save with sword and spear; for the battle *is* the LORD's, and He will give you into our hands." (1 Samuel 17:45-47 NKJV)

David was confident that two things would happen as a result of this victory. First, people all over the world would know about the God of Israel. He had yet to ascend to the throne and already he had a desire for Israel to be the light to the nations. Second, Israel would be reminded that God alone fought their battles.

David wasn't pretending to be anyone but himself. He was a shepherd boy from Bethlehem, which was exactly who Israel needed in that moment.

Rather than being behind, overlooked, and passed up, David was right on time. From this day forward, all of Israel would know his name.

When you're tempted to believe lies about your life, remember that you have nothing to prove. Your armor is enough. If you're a follower of Jesus, you are a redeemed child of God. Case closed, nothing left to say. You are part of a royal priesthood, a holy nation. You are a child of the King, and a warrior of the Most High God. Nothing and no one can change this, and you don't have to pretend to be something you're not. Comparison is intricately linked to disobedience because you aren't living with integrity. When running the race set before you is your focus, obedience is the result. Doing hard things will not seem insurmountable because you already know from Whom you receive your calling and the One who fights your battles.

POSITIONED FOR GREATNESS

Like David, you are uniquely equipped and prepared to write the story that God has for you. Imagine the daily grind for David as a shepherd. Most days, he just took care of slow, meandering sheep. He slept on the ground at night. He marched them in circles across the mountains and valleys. And at times, he risked his life to protect them. He could have easily assumed that it would have added up to nothing. It would have been natural to wonder if there was more to his life than the monotony of keeping sheep fed and safe.

While waiting for someone to notice, David remained faithful, became a marksman with the sling, and walked with his God. Every task you do, the education you get, the hours you put in, and the hardships you endure are adding up to the destiny God has for you. Remember the words of the boy who would become king. David wrote, "All he does is just and good, and all his commandments are trustworthy. They are forever true, to be obeyed faithfully and with integrity" (Psalm 111:7-8 NLT). Run your race.

QUESTIONS *for* TRANSFORMATION

1. When do you find yourself comparing yourself to others and their stories the most?

2. How have you seen comparison derail you in the past?

3. Make a sizable list of qualities that are unique to you. If you need help, ask some trusted peers and leaders. Now, how can you be faithful to carry out these unique elements of your design and purpose?

4. How can David's story of faithfulness encourage you today?

"If there is no struggle, there is no progress."

——FREDERICK DOUGLASS[32]

CHAPTER 13

MAKE LIFE A MASTERPIECE

2020 was a tough year. How's that for an understatement?

In many ways, it was a year marked by tremendous loss, upheaval, and speaking truth to power. But even in the toughest seasons, surprising joys could be found. Reflecting on my own life, there were lots of victories. Our family took advantage of the slower pace to enjoy small things in big ways. In years past, catching the latest kid's movie premiere required getting the whole family dressed and out the door, which is no small feat for a family of five. We'd drive across Indianapolis in search of the cheapest ticket, which usually meant watching the movie in a sticky seat with not-so-clean restrooms. We'd spend a small fortune at the concession stand on popcorn and sodas (or "pop" as we call it in Indiana). And, inevitably, at least one kid would require a bathroom break in an important part of the story.

So, when Pixar and Disney announced the release of *Soul* for Christmas Day 2020 on their Disney Plus streaming platform, there was much rejoicing in the Lunsford house—and our kids were also excited. We opened presents and ate our traditional Christmas breakfast, which includes homemade monkey bread in a Bundt pan (you should befriend my wife and ask for the recipe), and a southern grits-and-egg casserole that we picked up living in Mississippi. Once the festivities were over, the snuggling could begin. No longer would we have to venture out in the cold for a cheap ticket with crusty seats and over-priced popcorn. Late Christmas morning, with full hearts and over-stuffed bellies, it was time for enjoying the movie together. With the fire burning, we huddled underneath a pile of blankets, ready to watch *Soul.*

Once again, Pixar knocked it out of the park. The main character is Joe, an aspiring musician struggling to get his dream off the ground. Just as he's about to get his big break, daydreaming Joe suddenly dies in an accident. Throughout the story, Joe gets the privilege of seeing how he could live differently. Specifically, Joe learns to see better, to see the life he had differently. Joe isn't promised a different life. Rather, he discovers how to see the world that surrounds him with renewed awe and joy. At the end of the movie, Joe is given a second chance at living fully. And while we don't get to see what Joe does with it, we do see that his perspective has changed. When asked what he'll do with this unique opportunity, Joe responds, "I don't know, but I'm going to live every minute of it."[33]

What about us? What about you? Do you live every minute of this gift called life? I suspect that like most people, you've been knocked down a time or two. But I pray that this book is a part of opening your eyes to the wonder that God places before you. At the heart of Joe's renewed outlook is his newfound ability to see the miraculous in the everyday, often-overlooked joys in life. Because he could see the marvel in the mundane, he was released to live fully today. No longer was the win at some unreachable point in the future. Rather, he was understanding how to see the beauty inside the day he was living.

MY LIFE, MY MASTERPIECE

Legendary basketball coach and famous Hoosier John Wooden was known for more than his wins on the court. Without question, Wooden is revered as one of the greatest college basketball coaches ever (of course, the coach of my alma mater, Mike Krzyzewski of Duke University, is also up there in second place). And while you may disagree with me that Coach K is in second place, Wooden's ten national championships are without equal. He began his illustrious coaching career where I began my lackluster academic journey at Indiana State University, the home of Larry Bird!

Yet, Wooden's character, legacy, and leadership were even more remarkable than his athletic achievements. Renowned for his "Pyramid of Success," and many leadership mantras, Wooden's seven-point creed formed his core. And while all seven points are noteworthy, Point #3 has found its way into my life: "Make each day your masterpiece." It's realizing that God has given me a great gift, and I have the privilege, opportunity, and responsibility to live it fully. It's my life, my masterpiece. The Creator lovingly fashioned me, knows the hairs on my head, placed deep purpose in my soul, and outfitted me with divine faculties. It's not that I *can* live my greatest story; I *must*. Say it in your own heart: "my life, my masterpiece."

PERMISSION GRANTED

Everybody wants to be successful, but few people know when they've achieved it. The problem is not that only a few people have achieved success. Rather, most people have never defined what success is to them. Most people never make it past the comparison trap, so they're busy running down someone else's version of success while secretly wishing they could live a unique life. Dave Ramsey says it this way: "We buy things we don't need with money we don't have in order to impress people we don't like."[34] As a leader, I've learned that most people are seeking permission to break free from the norm to live an extraordinary life. Permission granted.

I love Mark Batterson's definition of success: ". . . doing the best you can, with what you have, where you are."[35] If you'll commit to this three-pronged approach, all bets are off. Seriously, no longer is success somewhere at some undefined place in the future. You can be successful today, right where you are, with the resources you already have. You have permission to be successful right now. Love your friends and family. Hit it out of the park at work. Live out your values and live for an audience of the One who matters only. If your goal is to finish each day a great steward before God, He rejoices over your life, and you don't need the approval or recognition of others. You can trust the psalmist, "Take delight in the LORD, and he will give you your heart's desires" (Psalm 37:4 NLT).

IS YOUR EYE HEALTHY?

Thank God for modern medicine. Each person in our household is reliant upon glasses or contacts to see. I can't imagine living hundreds of years ago before corrective lenses, and I still remember getting contacts in seventh grade. It was also "spirit day" at our school, and everyone wore hats and sports attire. I showed up without glasses and with a hat, and everyone wondered if I was a new kid at school. The spherical lenses that are manufactured to be placed in our frames, and the tiny little contacts we place on our eyes, dictate how we see the world around us.

Just as my prescription filters how I see things, the health of your spiritual eye directs how you see your life and the events that take place every day. Jesus said it this way: "'The eye is the lamp of the body. So, if your eye is healthy, your whole body will be full of light, but if your eye is bad, your whole body will be full of darkness'" (Matthew 6:22-23).

In short, *how* you see directly impacts *what* you see. Albert Einstein famously stated, "There are only two ways to live your life. One is as though nothing is a miracle. The other is as though everything is."[36] Which one are you? Or, let me ask you a better question: After today, how will you *choose* to see the world around you?

As wise as John Wooden was, making each day a masterpiece wasn't first his idea; it was God's. He literally makes each day a masterpiece. At the beginning, while God was forming the earth, He looked over His creation: "And God saw everything that he had made, and behold, it was very good" (Genesis 1:31).

When you set out to make each day successful and you see each day as a miracle, pretty soon, each day becomes a masterpiece. No longer are small things small. If each day is a miracle, then small things carry great weight. Sometimes the most spiritual thing you can do is start. Then, the next most spiritual thing you can do is show up again.

When I set out to write this book, it felt like a really big task. While I've felt called to write a book for some time, it was still a brand-new venture. I gave myself a goal of writing one thousand words. I didn't have to write the whole book to be successful. Just one thousand words. Then, I got up early the next day and did it again. And I kept on showing up early in my day. I emphasize "early" because I didn't have the margin to write a book, but I felt God was calling me to do it. So, four days a week, the alarm went off at 4:45 a.m. I made coffee, and I began writing. And most days, I hit one thousand words. Some days, I fell short, and other days, I overshot the target. Through it all, I kept hearing God's words in my spirit: "Do not despise these small beginnings, for the LORD rejoices to see the work begin . . ." (Zechariah 4:10 NLT).

God rejoices over you, too. God rejoices when you do little things like they carry great weight. God loves it when you love your friends and family well. God celebrates when you show up and do your job with your very best.

God cheers you on when you're not sure if anyone is watching but you live with integrity anyway. When you live with this perspective, you make it possible for God to show up in your life, turning the impossible into the possible.

KEEP DANCING

Even with this perspective, some days, you're going to miss it. Even the best hitters in baseball fail to reach first base seventy percent of the time. The best three-point shooters in basketball miss sixty percent of the time. Give yourself some grace if you miss the mark even half the time. What do you do? Keep going. Keep growing. Keep moving forward. Keep making progress.

As the spiritual leader of Israel, Samuel felt responsibility for the failures of King Saul. And despite the fact that Samuel warned Israel not to desire a king, he still grieved the rejection of Saul and the shame for Israel.

> Then Samuel went home to Ramah, and Saul returned to his house at Gibeah of Saul. Samuel never went to meet with Saul again, but he mourned constantly for him. And the Lord was sorry he had ever made Saul king of Israel.
>
> Now the Lord said to Samuel, "You have mourned long enough for Saul. I have rejected him as king of Israel, so fill your flask with olive oil and go to Bethlehem. Find a man named Jesse who lives there, for I have selected one of his sons to be my king" (1 Samuel 15:34-16:1 NLT).

God told Saul it was time to move forward. When Samuel advanced, David came on the scene. "So as David stood there among his brothers, Samuel took the flask of olive oil he had brought and anointed David with the oil. And the Spirit of the Lord came powerfully upon David from that day on" (1 Samuel 16:13 NLT). Samuel changed the game for David, and David changed the game for Israel. He was a man after God's heart (See 1 Samuel 13:14 NLT). Samuel couldn't mourn the past because God had a future to write. David would cause fear to grow in the hearts of enemy nations, and he would lead Israel with justice and equity (See 1 Chronicles 14:7; 18:14 NLT). He became Israel's greatest king, and in time, Jesus would come from his lineage.

There is a time to mourn, but there is also a time to dance (Ecclesiastes 3). When mourning is needed, know that God is close. "The Lord is close to the brokenhearted and saves those who are crushed in spirit" (Psalm 34:18 NIV). You do not mourn alone, and God stands ready to bring healing in your heart. God will meet you right where you are, and God loves you too much to let you stay there. So, when it's time to dance, God *will* pick you up, and God will enable you to move your feet to the rhythms of life. Keep dancing.

FAILURE ISN'T FINAL

I didn't even know that I could speak in front of a crowd. Until this moment, one hand would be more than enough to count the times that I had. Yet, something told me that I could do it. I *wanted* to do it. I asked for the opportunity.

For one week, the summer between my junior and senior year of high school, I ran the state of Indiana. Well, me and hundreds of other boys of the same age. Okay, we ran a fictitious realm called Hoosier Boys State, but we did so with all the class and wisdom you might expect from such a group of prodigious young men. Selected by our schools to represent them, we learned from great historians and political science teachers from across Indiana, and little by little, we ran for office and held them. I ran for Lieutenant Governor and missed out on the opportunity to represent our party in the general election by one vote. The other party's candidate ran circles around our contender in the debate, which let me know I had been given a large measure of grace by losing.

Not to be deterred, I volunteered to be our party's keynote speaker in front of the entire assembly at the state's convention. Now, I should remind you that I wasn't academically interested in high school. My uncle was part of our local American Legion. They made the nominations for local representation. I'm certain the only reason I was even invited is because of outright nepotism. Nonetheless, I decided to make the best of it.

I don't even remember why I thought I could do it, but I wanted the opportunity. I auditioned in front of party leadership and was given the mantle. I established a speech-writing team, and we prepared a powerful oration. The opposing party presented their platform first. By the time they finished, a dozen boys on the front row had taken off their shirts and waved them in the air while the crowd erupted in applause.

Now, it was our turn—specifically, my turn. I approached the microphone and let the noise die down. I began with a joke. I stated that it was common for nervous communicators to imagine the crowd in their underwear. I told the guys on the front row that I wasn't expecting it to actually happen, but that I appreciated them making me feel better. The place broke out in laughter and my over-zealous opponents took a seat. Then I proceeded to lay out our platform with great strength and with memorable statements. When I sat down, our opponents keynote speaker told me that I mopped the floor with him. Afterwards, my junior high history teacher, who was on the board for the organization, approached and told me that I did his heart good. That night, I knew that I was called to communicate. If I could do that in front of more than five hundred high school boys, I wondered what I could do in front of people who actually wanted to listen.

Now, compare this moment to the story I shared earlier about completely forgetting my message in front of a youth group. The forgotten message came a few years after my successful keynote speech. In one story, I was on top of the mountain. In the other story, beyond the valley, I was drowning in the river that was in the valley's floor. In one story, I was certain that I could not fail. In the other story, I was certain that failure would do me in. And the reality is that all of us will have those pinnacle moments. Oddly enough, they are usually followed by stumbling moments. But please hear this: Failure isn't final. Failure isn't the end of the story; it's often the beginning or even the way that leads us to something greater.

The writer of Hebrews knew this when they wrote, "Therefore, since we are surrounded by such a great cloud of witnesses, let us throw off everything that hinders and the sin that so easily entangles. And let us run with perseverance the race marked out for us . . ." (Hebrews 12:1 NIV). We look to the great cloud because they inspire us and lift us higher, but we also look to them and learn that even giants fall. In fact, they often fall harder. If you've stumbled, take heart; you're in great company. King David messed up big time. The Apostle Paul would call himself the worst of sinners. As we saw in Chapter Nine, the Prophet Elijah participated in some of the greatest miracles ever recorded, and he also prayed that God would take his life. They aren't perfect, which means they are the perfect people to remind us that failure isn't final. If you struggle moving past your past, let the great cloud of witness remind you that your failure isn't final.

GOD IS A GOOD FATHER

As a dad, I couldn't remain on the sidelines without helping. There's a fine line of knowing when to let your kids handle a challenge on their own and knowing when they need you. My daughter, Ella, is a fierce competitor. Seriously, regardless of the game you're playing, you want Ella on your team. She will find a way to win. So, when Katie and I realized that we had accidentally signed her up for a co-ed soccer travel league, we decided to let her stay on the team. We had our concerns. At that time, Ella was small for her age. We liked to call her "fun size." At the first practice, we quickly noticed that some of the boys were literally twice her size. "If anyone could find a way to excel," we reasoned, "it was Ella." Never one to back down from a challenge, she jumped right in. I'm not even sure if she realized how big some of the boys were.

In one of the first tournaments of the year, we played another co-ed team from Indianapolis, and somehow the boys seemed even bigger. As early elementary students, most of them were still learning how to use their bodies and play the game. One boy from the other team had discovered how to wind up and kick the ball from midfield. In fact, it was his only move. Wherever he was on the field, regardless of where he was trying to kick, and despite other kids in his path, he wound up and kicked it as though the World Cup was at stake. Somehow, I knew this was going to end badly for Ella.

Sure enough, Ella decided to play defense against this man in a boy's body, and his kick turned into a heat-seeking missile destined for her face. When the ball hit her, the crowd gasped, but the players kept on—even Ella. Somehow, she held it together. I would have been in the fetal position sucking my thumb. Besides, that's what soccer players are supposed to do. When they writhe in pain on the ground, they're hoping the referee will start passing out yellow cards. Ella didn't play *that* game; she kept it all in.

But then it happened again. I'm not kidding. Less than five minutes later, it was déjà vu. The man-child received a pass, Ella went to defend him, he wound up to kick, and then attempted to score from midfield. Rather than reaching the goal forty yards away, it smacked Ella in the face. Again. She held it together for a moment, but then decided it wasn't worth it and the tears came out. The coach substituted her out, and there she sat on the bench. My sweet little Ella, sobbing on the bench, holding her face, by herself. What would you do?

I stood to my feet and Katie looked at me. After years of marriage, I know the looks and this one meant, "Are you sure she wants you? Don't embarrass her." I wasn't sure what she wanted, but I wanted to hold her in my arms for the next hour and then kick the ball in the boy's face. Luckily, I composed myself and briskly walked around the pitch to the bench. I put my arm around her for a moment, and then I looked her in the eyes and said, "I'm so proud of you. You are so tough." A couple moments later, she looked at the coach and declaratively stated, "I'm ready," and she went back into the game.

After the match, I asked her if I embarrassed her and if she wanted me to come to her. Ella said, "Dad, I did want you. After you came over, I felt much better." Ella knew I was there for her, and she found strength in my presence. She knew she was loved and was encouraged to get back in the game.

There will be times when you get smacked in the face by life. There are lots of pressures, resistance, and worries in this world. But know this: You are deeply loved by your heavenly Father, and when you feel beat down, He stands ready to hold you close, look you in the eyes, and give you strength to get back in the game. When you know Whose you are, you can be confident in who you are. You don't have to be more; you are more than enough with your identity in Christ. You're a child of God, and nothing further needs to be proved.

As a dad, I don't always get it right. However, there are times when I nail it. I intuitively know when my kids need an extra push, a word of encouragement, or just a long hug. God is your Good Father; He knows what you need, and He provides for you. I know that sounds cliché, but lock this in your heart. When you are in your moments of greatest need, you'll be tempted to do it all in your own strength and find solutions that are less than God's best. Instead, choose to run to God, who knows what you need and is ready to provide.

The truth is that so often when we fail, we allow our shame to drive us away from people. The Bible actually teaches us that when we open up ourselves with other followers of Jesus, it brings healing in our lives (See James 5:16).

Maybe you've been running and wandering, and you've felt lost, alone, and desperate. You've been looking all around, but I'm telling you that God's been next to you the whole time. It's why the psalmist writes, "Your Spirit is everywhere I go. I cannot escape your presence. If I go up to heaven, you will be there. If I go down to the place of death, you will be there. If I go east where the sun rises or go to live in the west beyond the sea, even there you will take my hand and lead me. Your strong right hand will protect me" (Psalm 139:7-10 ERV). If you're depleted, it's time to let God fill you up.

THE LORD WILL FULFILL HIS PURPOSE FOR YOU

Much of the good news about making each day your masterpiece is that it doesn't all depend on you. There will be times that you'll give up on yourself, but God doesn't give up on you. Your faith will fail, but God won't. God made you, and God knows the purpose He placed inside of you.

Often, failure is an opportunity. If we leverage our mistakes, failure becomes the open door for us to experience God's steadfast belief in us. God loves you just as much in your failures as He does in your successes. God's love isn't fleeting. God's love isn't based on your performance. God won't desert you when you're at your lowest. God will find you, pick you up, dust you off, and send you back in the game because even when you give up on yourself, God will not give up on you. God loves you. God put purpose in you. Failure isn't final; it's often the door we'll walk through on the way to God's biggest plans for our lives. It's why the psalmist could confidently proclaim, "The Lord will fulfill his purpose for me; your steadfast love, O Lord, endures forever" (Psalm 138:8).

As you march toward living out your greatest story, don't allow failures and missteps to derail you. Rather, let them fuel you to experience God at new levels. Obstacles aren't the end; they are often the way. Your best days are ahead. God will help you see what He sees in you. You are redeemed and loved, bestowed with great purpose and created with divine destiny. Allow God to renew your heart and get you back in the game. There's too much at stake. Please don't settle. Make today a masterpiece. Declare it: "My life, my masterpiece!"

QUESTIONS *for* TRANSFORMATION

1. As you begin to consider your next steps toward living your greatest story, which ones feel the biggest?

2. How can the mindset of making today a master-piece make the steps attainable?

3. If Samuel continued to mourn Saul, there would have never been a David. Is there a past failure or mistake that is preventing you from stepping into your future?

4. How does knowing that God is a Good Father and that He will fulfill His purpose for your life help you stay on course and focus on today?

"In our abandonment we give ourselves over to God just as God gave Himself for us, without any calculations. The consequences of abandonment never enter into our outlook because our life is taken up in Him."

——OSWALD CHAMBERS[37]

WHERE'S YOUR WEIGHT?

On a recent family vacation to Disney World, I was reminded of the importance of choosing wisely where you place your weight. The girls and I were in line for Big Thunder Mountain, one of our all-time favorites. I don't know about you, but when I'm waiting in lines at amusement parks, I'm always looking for a place to lean. A spot to place my weight. My back and feet are aching, and my legs are tired.

At one particular area of the line, there was a short wall with a window above it. Just as I was leaning back, the line started to move, and the girls began to walk forward. The only problem was that I didn't stop going backwards. What I didn't realize is that when I leaned back, I had hit a lever. I was not leaning against a short immovable wall; I was actually leaning against a short doorway with a big lever. When my butt hit the lever, I kept falling out the door and almost fell off Big Thunder Mountain. Luckily, I eventually caught myself and only made a small fool of myself. I still laugh, picturing that the girls would have turned around and I would have vanished, having fallen off Big Thunder Mountain. It matters where you put your weight.

Where's your weight?

Now, I'm not asking how much you weigh. I'm asking, "Where's your trust?" Are you leaning against something that's going to move, like your own wisdom and understanding, and that of the world? Or are you leaning against an unchanging, immovable wall like God's wisdom upon which you can place all your weight, all your trust, and all your obedience? No matter how hard it is to trust, you will never regret placing all your weight on God. God is worthy of your trust. God is worthy of your faith. God can hold up all your weight. What are you leaning on today? Where's your weight?

LEAN ON GOD

One of the earliest verses that I learned and memorized after becoming a follower of Jesus is Proverbs 3:5-6. Some of you may know it too. It says this: "Trust in the LORD with all your heart and lean not on your own understanding; in all your ways submit to him, and he will make your paths straight" (NIV). It's a wonderful verse written on walls and plaques. But let's be real: Most people, even followers of Jesus, don't trust God with all their hearts. We want God to make our paths straight, but we don't submit to God in all our ways.

In reality, we often give God *parts* of our heart. We submit to God in *some* of our ways. But what would happen if you made a commitment to daily give God everything? What if you allowed God to grow you in your faith in new areas of your life? Maybe for you, it'll be in your relationships. For someone else, maybe it's time to begin trusting God with finances. For another, God has been knocking on your heart to be a voice of hope in your daily sphere of influence; at school, at work, or in your neighborhood. I don't know what it is for you, but what if you gave God access to more of your heart? What if your paths became straight because you learned to submit to God in a new area of your life?

I love the imagery that Solomon gives us in this passage of Proverbs. He tells us not to lean on our own understanding, but to lean on God. God is much bigger than us. God has a significantly greater vision than we do. The Hebrew word for lean is *sa an* (pronounced shaw-anne), and it means "to trust, to lean on, or to support." It's a word picture, meaning "where you place your weight." If you lean against something, you're trusting it to hold you. Are you trusting in your own wisdom, vision, and strength, or have you placed all your weight on God?

DEEP WATERS

As you finish reading this book and take steps to write your own story, I want to share with you two prayers that I've learned.[38] To do this, I want to unfold the transformation of Simon in Luke 5. Just like us, Simon had to learn and grow and get better. The disciples faced real-life situations where they'd have to trust God, even when it didn't make sense. These two prayers will help you grow in trusting God with more and more of your heart.

One morning, a large crowd was pressing in on Jesus as He was standing by a lake. Jesus wanted to teach them, but the crowd was pushing Him into the water. Two boats were sitting nearby, and Jesus hopped in one of them. The fishermen who owned the boats were nearby, cleaning their nets. They had caught nothing all night and were sulking off to the side. Jesus asked one of them, named Simon, to put out a little into the water. Jesus sat down in the boat and began to teach the crowd.

"And when he had finished speaking, he said to Simon, 'Put out into the deep and let down your nets for a catch.' And Simon answered, 'Master, we toiled all night and took nothing!'" (Luke 5:4-5)

As Jesus taught, He told Simon to "put out a little," but as He finished up with His teaching, Jesus said, "put out into the deep."

Jesus wanted to grow Simon in the area of trust, so He told him to "put out into the deep waters." I believe Jesus is saying that to you as you finish reading today. "I want to grow you in your trust of Me, so I need you to put out into deep waters. We can't stay close to the shore. You can't lean on Me with all your heart in the shallow waters. You've got to push out." To write your greatest story, you can't stay where you are. You're going to have to venture out into the deep waters and begin taking some risks. It's time to lay hold of what Jesus laid hold of in you (See Philippians 3).

Then, Jesus told Simon to let down his nets. And do you remember Simon's response? "We worked our butts off all night, and we caught nothing!" There's actually an exclamation: "Nothing!"

Let's put ourselves in Simon's mind for a moment. He respected Jesus. In fact, he respected Jesus enough to let Him in the boat in the first place and to put out a little while Jesus taught. But now Jesus was giving fishing tips. Jesus wasn't the fisherman; Simon was. It's likely that he came from a long line of fishermen, and he probably knew those waters better than most. He put in a full night of work and this Rabbi had the audacity to say, "Let's go fishing!" There were no fish to catch. They were already cleaning their nets and calling it a day. They were tired. They were frustrated and had already thrown in the towel, and then this teacher told them to try again. And this is important to realize: Jesus wasn't concerned with the fish or fishing. Jesus wanted to teach Simon about trusting Him with all his weight.

Jesus will also call you out into the deep and invite you to do things that don't always make sense. God will ask you to place your trust in Him, and it will push you to your limits because you can't get your mind around it. It's all over the scriptures. Jesus will say things like, ". . . do not worry about tomorrow because tomorrow will worry about itself" (Matthew 6:34 NIV). This is super easy to quote to someone else, but it can be really tough to live out in your own life. You've probably thought, *Somebody needs to worry about* something! *Haven't you looked around? Things are a mess!*

Or Jesus will say, "Bless those who persecute you" (Matthew 5:11, paraphrased). Again, it's easy advice to pass on, but it's really tough when your work environment is toxic. The Bible teaches us to tithe, which means we give the first ten percent of our income back to God before we do anything else. Sounds like a wonderful thing, but then you think about what you could do with that ten percent. Then, you're reminded of Solomon's words earlier: "Lean not on your own understanding." *Okay*, you think, *but who's going to pay the bills?*

PRAYER #1: HELP ME TRUST

Sometimes, what God asks us to do can feel unreasonable. How do you place your weight on God, who you can't see and you can't always feel? This leads to the first prayer I want you to take with you as you begin to walk boldly with God:

"Lord, help me to trust You, even when I don't understand You."

You can quietly pray that in your own heart right now, or maybe you need to pray it loudly:

"Lord, help me to trust You, even when I don't understand You."

 In essence, this is what Simon does.

"I don't understand You, Lord, but I'm still going to obey You."

Jesus asked Simon to let down the nets. And here was all of Simon's response: "'Master, we toiled all night and took nothing! But at your word I will let down the nets'" (Luke 5:5)

In other words, "I don't understand it, but I'll still obey You. This doesn't make sense to me, but because it's You, I'll obey." In fact, Simon teaches us that you don't have to understand completely to obey God fully. You don't have to know how the story ends to keep turning the pages.

When we think of obeying God, we usually think of the big things, like moving to a new city or starting a new career—and those are areas of our lives where we definitely want God's input—but I've often found that when God is growing our trust, He starts with the small things. Let down the nets. And here's what's so amazing: Often, the small acts of obedience lead to some of the biggest results and some of the most incredible miracles.

SIMPLE OBEDIENCE, BIG RESULTS

It's hard to recount all the times over the years that something like this happens to me—when someone will come to my mind and memory, and then I'll send a quick text of encouragement to let them know that I'm praying for them. Over and over, people will text me back, "How did you know? I really needed prayer and you reminded me of God's love for me!" It was a simple act of obedience that meant so much to someone else.

I love a story that a friend of mine would share. He's a pediatric dentist, and he loves to care for the families. He was consulting with a family when he felt prompted by the Holy Spirit. My friend and his wife were attending a Christian marriage conference soon, and he felt like he was supposed to invite them and pay their way. Now, he was afraid that the invitation and the offer to pay might offend them, perhaps suggesting that he had more money or that their marriage needed help. He didn't think either of those things; he just felt prompted to bless them. So, he asked anyway. They were actually excited at the opportunity and decided to attend. My friend ran into the husband at the conference and in tears, the husband shared how he and his wife had recently begun to talk about divorce and didn't know how to get help. When my friend invited them to a marriage conference, they knew that God was with them and that they couldn't give up on the marriage. One simple act of obedience can have big results.

LET DOWN YOUR NETS

Do you remember what Jesus told Simon to do?

"Let down the nets."

It's a simple action, and it didn't make much sense since they had already tried all night, but Simon obeyed. And what appears small to us is monumental for Simon. In physically letting go of the nets, Simon was figuratively grabbing hold of Jesus. He was transferring his trust from his identity and profession as a fisherman, and he was becoming a follower of Jesus. Instead of trusting in his own ways and wisdom, Simon could now lean on Jesus. He could place his weight on the trustworthiness of Christ.

Think back to Proverbs 3:5-6. Do you remember the first phrase of that passage?

"Trust in the Lord."

Simon was learning to let down the nets, which represented his own wisdom and ways. He was learning to hold on to Jesus and lean on *His* ways. It's moving to a place of letting go of your own understanding, your own plans and desires, and your own will and comfort. It's laying hold of Jesus, the Rock, who will never let you down, and the Anchor, who will never let you go.

Anything else that used to bring an illusion of security begins to fade in the presence and strength of Almighty God. It's holding onto the promises of God: You never leave me; when I draw near to You, You draw near to me; He's close to the broken hearted; He saves those who are crushed in spirit; He's my refuge and strength; He's my help in times of trouble!

In order to hold onto the goodness of God, you will have to let down some nets (some old ways of thinking) and begin leaning on the faithfulness of a God that loves you beyond your comprehension.

"Lord, help me to trust you even when I don't understand."

PRAYER #2: HELP ME SURRENDER

Simon didn't know the outcome, but he trusted. The outcome isn't your responsibility, it is God's. Trust and obedience are your responsibility. God will invite you to greater trust. And what you'll discover is that big miracles often follow small acts of trust. In the story, Jesus says "let down your nets." Simon obeyed, and watch what transpires:

"And when they had done this, they enclosed a large number of fish, and their nets were breaking. They signaled to their partners in the other boat to come and help them. And they came and filled both the boats, so that they began to sink" (Luke 5:6-7).

This leads to the second prayer that will guide you as we write your greatest story:

"Lord, help me surrender my story to You."

I suspect that you may need to pray that in your heart right now:

"Lord, help me surrender my story to You."

LET GO OF THE NETS

There's a significant transformation taking place with Simon in this story. He respects Jesus, and he's listening to Jesus. He has small acts of obedience: letting Jesus use his boat, putting out a little, going into deep waters, then letting down the nets. Then, after all these small steps, Simon's eyes were opened. He caught so many fish that his nets could not contain them. He was a fisherman, but he had never had a catch like that. He shouted and motioned to his friends, and then both boats were filling up so much that the boats started to sink.

Simon was realizing that Jesus was more than the average Rabbi; He was more than a prophet. Jesus was the Messiah they had been looking forward to for generations. And Simon's response is so real and so raw.

But when Simon Peter saw it, he fell down at Jesus's knees, saying, "Depart from me, for I am a sinful man, O Lord." For he and all who were with him were astonished at the catch of fish that they had taken, and so also were James and John, sons of Zebedee, who were partners with Simon. And Jesus said to Simon, "Do not be afraid; from now on you will be catching men." (Luke 5:8-10)

Simon was in awe of Jesus, and he realized that on his own, he couldn't stand in the presence of the Holy One. But Jesus said, "Simon, I've got such great plans for your life. You've been working for fish, but I'm going to transform your talents and now you'll fish for people." Jesus called him to greater trust and new heights, but it began with small actions. Then, watch the transformation that emerges: "And when they had brought their boats to land, they left everything and followed him" (v. 11).

The story began with Simon and his fishing partners cleaning their nets after a disappointing night of fishing. They were fishermen; these were their nets and their boats. This was their livelihood. In the middle of the story, they let *down* their nets, but they never let *go* of them. The nets had a rope tied to them so they could pull in the catch. But in this last scene, they don't just let *down* the nets. They let *go* of their nets. At first, they let *down* their nets; one small act of trust. But now they *leave* their nets behind—a big act of trust, which will lead to an even greater catch and an even higher calling. All their hard work, all their security, all their planning for the future, left behind to trust Jesus with what was ahead.

What are the nets in your life? Where is God asking you to let down the nets? Where is Jesus inviting you to small acts of trust? What areas of your life have you been leaning on your own understanding? What parts of your life have you yet to place your weight on Jesus? You're leaning on a door that's moving, and Jesus is inviting you to place your weight on Him.

Maybe God's inviting you to let go of the nets. You've been making your plans. You've been working it out your own way. You've told God, "If you'll just provide this, or move that, then I can take it from there."

And Jesus is inviting us to lean *wholly* on Him, to give Him *all* our weight, *all* our trust, and to say, "I'm letting go of my plans. I'm trusting You in every area, not just some areas."

God is inviting some to let *down* their nets and trust Him with a next step. For others, God is inviting them to let *go* of their nets, to leave behind their way of doing something, and go all-in with Him.

GOD IS WORTHY OF YOUR TRUST

And if I can leave you with a parting thought, it's this: God is worthy of your trust, and God will never let you down. His understanding is greater than yours. His vision is higher than yours. His love for you is beyond what you can comprehend. His goodness is such that He sent His own son to die on a cross for *you*! You can trust in the Lord with *all* your heart and lean not on your *own* understanding. You can submit to Him in *all* of your ways and God *will* make your paths straight.

David wrote in Psalm 20:7: "Some trust in chariots and some in horses, but we trust in the name of the Lord our God" (ESV). Do you see the difference? As the king, David led a nation and commanded an army. As he surveyed the other nations, he said "that some trust in what they can see, but I place my weight on God." David makes clear: "I lean on my God. They trust in their mighty chariots and horses; I trust my God. Their hope, their faith, their trust is in the things they possess, but my hope, my faith, and my trust is in the name of the Lord Who loves me, fights for me, and is worthy of my weight. He's getting it all."

So, what about you? Where's your weight? What are you leaning on? Some trust in the stock market, while others trust in the strength of their company's contribution to the economy. Some lean on their bank account, others in their medical report. If the events of 2020 taught us anything, it's that we have far less control over our lives than we thought. And while we don't have the power to control everything in the world, we always have the opportunity to surrender to a God that's over it all.

Will you hold on to the illusion of control or will you hold on to the Anchor that will never be shaken? Is your faith in who holds office or in the One that sits on the throne? Some trust in chariots and some trust in horses, but you? You're going to trust in the name of the Lord, your God.

LET YOUR FAITH SOAR

Get your hopes up. Get your faith up. Let trust arise in you today. Think about Simon and the other fishermen. When did their miracle come? When did Jesus step into their story? When they had given up hope and when they were frustrated. When they had tried all their skills, and all their talents were exhausted. All they knew to do had been tried. Then Jesus stepped in at the end of a frustrating day. The miracle came when hope had been lost.

I don't know where you've given up hope, but I pray that you'll hear this: Jesus wants to meet you right there. I don't know what it is for you, but I want you to know, from the depths of my soul: God loves you. God has plans for you. God isn't done with your story. He has joy waiting for you. He has hope in your future. He has good things coming that you can't even see today. He's good, and He's in control. He has more for you. He's still with you.

Do not give up. Do not throw in the towel. Keep striving for your greatest story. Keep pressing on. Lay hold of that for which Jesus Christ laid hold of you. You can trust God even when it doesn't make sense. You can surrender your story to God and trust that He'll fulfill His purpose for your life. You're placing all your weight, all your trust in God. If you receive it, will you pray this with me?

Father, help me to put my trust in You. Enable me to believe that You want to see my life soar, and to see that it can when I trust you with it all. Wake me up to seize the moments before me, to reclaim the truth of who I am in You, and to passionately pursue my God-given purpose. Empower me to move with purpose, to persevere when I feel like quitting, to act in faith as You put wind in my sails, and to stay close to You when it feels like I'm falling behind.

Father, I want to make a difference with my life. So, help me to focus on a fight worthy of my life, to pursue it with self-giving courage, and to trust You beyond my comfort zones. Cultivate character within me; guide me to gratefulness, generosity, integrity, and wholeness. Lead me to be a generous leader.

Father, as I begin to take big strides, help me to run my race rather than comparing my life to others. As I trust You with it all, my desire is to present my life as a masterpiece each and every day.

In Jesus' Name, Amen.

ACKNOWLEDGMENTS

The stories and insights comprised in this book are only possible thanks to more people than I can possibly mention. Thank you for enriching my life and the opportunity to share. Several chapters would be needed to adequately appreciate you all. You know who you are because I've had the privilege of telling most of you in person.

Words like acknowledgement and gratitude are simultaneously apt and insufficient when attempting to express thankfulness to my Lord and Savior. Before Jesus, I was lost, hurting, selfish, and confused. I desired a life of meaning but had no idea where to begin. Through the Holy Spirit, Jesus sought me. A friend invited me to church. A Spirit-filled pastor opened the scriptures to me. My life has not been the same. I am saved, redeemed, and filled with purpose because the Son of Heaven relinquished His throne, took up a cross, borrowed a tomb, and broke the gates of death and Hell forever. Once isolated from my Maker because of my sin, through Jesus I've gained access to my Father. This book is an attempt to help others learn to follow Him wholeheartedly.

Acknowledgement must also begin with my beautiful bride, Katie. We had no idea back in high school of the adventures ahead of us. Your investment in me and our journey is written on every page of this book. You are my best friend, my walking partner, and the personification of God's extravagant kindness to me. You are divinely appointed to mother our children, and the world is better because of your investment in them. Thank you for choosing me and the life we have together! When people discover how to act courageously, they'll do so because of your deep faith in God.

Thank you, Ava for letting me tell our story and for letting me learn how to become a parent to you. I love seeing the world through your eyes, and this book is a testament to the potential you see in all people. You teach me and all who know you what it is to be fiercely loved and to reach for our highest purpose. Keep riding the wind of God; I'll put wind in your sails as you bring light to the darkness of this world.

Thank you, Ella, for making every story that you're a part of immeasurably better, especially mine! Every day you teach me what it looks like to meet all challenges with excellence, to savor all things, and to express deep kindness to others. This book will inspire people to wholeheartedly live their greatest story because you help our family live ours. Keep running with God; I'll be your running partner as your pure heart illuminates the world around.

Thank you, Aidan for making every moment richer, bringing laughter and joy, and giving a deeper appreciation. It's no wonder why everyone wants to be around you. You make us all feel that we are made for more. When people learn to serve others and reflect God's character, it'll be because I see it in you every day. Keep allowing the fire of God's love to burn brightly in your soul; I'll be in your corner as you guide others to experience great victories.

Thank you, Mark Batterson, for reminding me that if only my children (and someday grandchildren) read this book, it will be more than worth it.

Your encouragement and guidance brought my dream to life. Thank you for being in my corner and for extending your credibility to me. Keep passionately pursuing Jesus; the rest of us are getting caught up in your fire.

Thanks to Esther Fedorkevich, Mariah Swift, and the entire Fedd Agency team! Thank you for believing in me, this book, and all that's ahead. I'm grateful for your guidance every step of the way. Moreover, thank you Linda Alila and Abbey McLaughlin for your influential insights and editing.

Thanks to Alan Briggs for your early coaching, encouragement, and feedback. Your experience and friendship were instrumental at the onset of this project, and your wisdom still resonates.

Thanks to Mike Ruman for helping more people experience the message of *Made for More*.

I want to thank my parents, Tom and Julie, for their consistent love and support. You both were dealt difficult cards, but that didn't stop you from building a beautiful life. Thank you for teaching me to never settle.

I want to thank faithful encouragers and supporters: Justin and Lisa Rhodes, Chris and Amber Tincher, and Jim and Lottie McCallister.

Thank you to the countless leaders that have done the difficult work of discipling a younger version of me, notably Dave Hoskins for introducing me to Jesus, Derek Mull for always being a phone call away, Steve Saccone for inviting me to begin a great adventure, and Mark Waltz for giving me permission to follow God's unique design.

Thank you to the faith-filled people of Echo Church. Together, we wrote the chapters of this book. Your tireless commitment to echo God's love inspires me still. Thank you to Connection Pointe Christian Church for believing in our dream, carrying hope forward, and building upon our foundation.

Thank you to Aaron Brockett and Traders Point Christian Church for empowering me to keep pursuing God's call. You have breathed new life into our souls and we're expectant for all that God has ahead. We're honored to carry the baton of leadership with you to remove unnecessary barriers that keep people from Jesus in Indianapolis and beyond.

ENDNOTES

INTRODUCTION

1   Frederick Buechner, *Wishful Thinking: A Seeker's ABC* (San Francisco: Harper, 1993), 119.

CHAPTER 1

2   Brian Thomsen, ed. *The Man in the Arena: The Selected Writings of Theodore Roosevelt, a Reader.* (New York: Forge, 2003).

CHAPTER 2

3   Maya Angelou, *Letter To My Daughter* (New York, NY: Random House, 2008), xii.

4   2005 study published by the National Science Foundation.

5   For a tremendous resource on developing a new way of thinking, read Craig Groeschel's *Winning The War In Your Mind: Change Your Thinking, Change Your Life* (Grand Rapids: Zondervan, 2021).

CHAPTER 3

6   Helen Keller, *Let Us Have Faith* (Garden City, NY: Doubleday and Company, 1946), 50-51.

7   C. S. Lewis, *The Problem of Pain* (New York: HarperOne, 1996), 34–35.

CHAPTER 4

8   Rene J. Dubos, *Louis Pasteur: Free Land of Science* (Boston: Little, Brown and Company, 1950), 63.

CHAPTER 5

9   Marian Wright Edelman, "Kids First," (*Mother Jones,* Volume 16, Number 31, Foundation For National Progress, (May-June 1991), 77.

10 Thomas Merton, *Thoughts In Solitude* (New York: Farrar, Straus and Giroux, 1999), p. 79.

CHAPTER 6

11 T.S. Eliot, *Collected Poems, 1909-1962* (London: Faber and Faber, 1963), p. 40.

CHAPTER 7

12 Carmine Gallo, *The Storyteller's Secret: From TED Speakers to Business Legends, Why Some Ideas Catch On and Others Don't* (New York: St. Martin's, 2016), 114.

13 Mark Batterson, *All In: You Are One Decision Away from a Totally Different Life* (Grand Rapids: Zondervan, 2013), 35-37.

CHAPTER 8

14 Erwin McManus, *Uprising: A Revolution of the Soul* (Nashville: Thomas Nelson, 2006), 101.

15 Time Staff. "The Great Survivor: Ernest Shackleton," *Time*, September 12, 2003. (accessed August 12, 2021). http://content.time.com/time/specials/packages (CMOS 14.18)/article/0,28804,1981290_1981354,00.html

CHAPTER 9

16 Thomas À Kempis, *The Imitation of Christ* (Chicago: Moody, 2007), 75.

17 *Study Bible* (Wheaton, IL: Crossway, 2008), 398.

18 John C. Maxwell, *Learning From The Giants: Life and Leadership Lessons from The Bible* (New York: Faith Words, 2014), 6.

19 Ibid. 10.

20 Craig Groeschel, "God With Us; In the Wilderness," accessed May 25, 2021. https://www.life.church/media/god-with-us/in-the-wilderness

CHAPTER 10

21 James Merritt, *52 Weeks Through the Psalms: A One-Year Journey of Prayer and Praise* (Eugene, OR: Harvest House, 2017), 92.

22 Richard B. Gunderman, *We Make A Life By What We Give* (Bloomington, IN: Indiana University Press, 2008), 56. This quote is often attributed to Winston Churchill.

23 Robert Morris' teachings on giving have been instrumental in forming my own thoughts. For this section, see Chapter Two in *The Blessed Life: Unlocking the Rewards of Generous Living* (Grand Rapids: Baker Publishing Group, 2016).

24 Often, people think that the principle of tithing is only found in the Old Testament. In fact, Jesus reminds us not to neglect the tithe (Matthew 23:23; Luke 11:42). Religious leaders claimed they had been following God's Law because they tithed. Jesus agreed that they should not neglect the tithe; it is baseline obedience to God. But He added that they had forgotten to love people. Yes, they should tithe, and they should love the people they're supposed to be serving, rather than heaping rules upon them.

25 Mike Holmes, "What Would Happen If the Church Tithed?" RELEVANT. June 15, 2021. https://relevantmagazine.com/faith(CMOS 14.18)/church/what-would-happen-if-church-tithed/.

26 Van Gogh Museum of Amsterdam: Vincent van Gogh Letters, Letter number: 274. Letter from Vincent van Gogh, Location: The Hague, Letter to: Theo van Gogh, Date: October 22, 1882. Van Gogh Letters Project database of the Van Gogh Museum. (Accessed vangoghletters. org on August 20, 2021: http://vangoghletters.org/vg/letters/let274/letter.html)

27 Saint Augustine (of Hippo) & Michael P. Foley, *Confessions*, (Indianapolis, IN: Hackett, 2006), 3.

CHAPTER 12

28 Bob Goff, *Live in Grace, Walk in Love: A 365-Day Journey* (Nashville: Thomas Nelson, 2019), 221.

29 Bob Goff, *Dream Big: Know What You Want, Why You Want It, and What You're Going to Do About It* (Nashville, Thomas Nelson, 2020), 83.

30 Malcom Gladwell, *David and Goliath: Underdogs, Misfits, and the Art of Battling Giants* (New York City: Little, Brown & Company, 2015), 9.

31 Ibid. 12, citing Dohrenwend article.

CHAPTER 13

32 David W. Blight, *Frederick Douglass: Prophet of Freedom* (New York: Simon & Schuster, 2020), 285.

33 Pete Docter, dir. [Soul.] 2020; Burbank, CA: Walt Disney Studios Motion Pictures, Disney Plus.

34 Dave Ramsey, *The Total Money Makeover: A Proven Plan for Financial Fitness* (Nashville: Thomas Nelson, 2009), 31.

35 Mark Batterson, *Win The Day: 7 Daily Habits to Help you Stress Less & Accomplish More* (Colorado Springs: Multnomah, 2020), 107.

36 Batterson, 109.

EPILOGUE

37 Stephen Arterburn, *100 Days to Freedom from Depression* (Carol Stream, IL: Tyndale House Publishers, 2021), Day 61.

38 These prayers and the arc of this epilogue were assisted with thoughts from Craig Groeschel, especially the message "Can You Trust God?" found at https://www.life.church/media/in-god-we-trust/can-you (CMOS 14.18)-trust-god/.